First Job Savvy

First Job
Savvy

GET A JOB, START YOUR CAREER

Denise P Kalm
DPK Coaching

ISBN: 1515371468
ISBN 13: 9781515371465

Contents

This book is dedicated to my young coaching clients and their parents. Working with them has inspired this book.

Introduction

"Control your own destiny
or someone else will."
JACK WELCH, RETIRED GE CEO

Parents and other adults may have told you about the 'career fairs' that proliferated at college campuses in the '60s and '70s. Companies, hungry for new talent, set up booths in the largest space a university had to offer and interview-blitzed seniors, waving good starting salaries and perks with abandon. With a limited 'catch' available, the hordes of employee fishermen were hungry and competitive. It was a great time to be looking for a position.

That was then. This is now. Tight job markets have transformed the 'ole fishing hole' into a seething mass of hungry fish hoping that just one lure will drop, offering a treat. But almost no one is fishing. Instead of being wooed, most college grads find themselves in the maddening position of trying to simply cling to the part-time jobs they held during college, competing with teens for minimum wage. This isn't your parents' job market.

Her new-minted geology degree still fresh from the printer, Georgia knew that landing an internship would be a snap. Top of her class and female, she felt she offered a compelling package, one that any of several select employers would find irresistible. With confidence, she launched herself into the world of online job applications, applying for as many as 20 jobs in a week. After a month of receiving only auto-rejections, she began to wonder what she was doing wrong. Still, the method she had been using was the same as all her fellow graduates. Georgia skillfully navigated the web, finding not just the usual companies to apply to, but others, where she expected her fellow students might not try. Still, she didn't even land an interview.

Just as many have abandoned landlines, 8-tracks and other 20th century technologies, so must we abandon the old methods for landing a career job. Modern methods are a start, but it won't be enough when jobs are scarce and applicants are rife. What you need is an edge, a way to stand out among the thousands of applicants. **First Job Savvy – Find a Job, Start Your Career** will help you differentiate yourself.

Once you land the job, you'll find expectations differ significantly from what you experienced with part-time, college or high school jobs. By understanding the 'rules of the road,' you can ensure your success going forward.

First Job Savvy is divided into three sections: Preparing to Apply, Landing the Job and Keeping the Job. Depending on where you are now in your career path, you may feel drawn to certain sections. This book will act as a useful guide for your first few years in the work world.

Stories inspired by real-world job seekers are included to help make the points real.[1] Where appropriate, exercises will be offered. You'll get the most from this book if you complete them. The book finishes with a Resources section listing some good sites to consider.

As a coach, I work with people of various ages and at different points in their career. This helps me understand that the techniques and approaches I apply to coaching experienced workers need to be adapted to the different challenges faced by people in the beginning of their career. However, an invariant rule is that you get out of coaching what you put in. You have educated yourself to be ready to step confidently onto the career stage. What you do now could make a significant difference in how you will succeed over the next 40 years. It's worth your best effort.

Let's get started.

---

1 Names and stories included here are fictional and any relation to a person or situation is purely coincidental.

Preparing to Apply

CHAPTER 1

Assess Yourself

"Work is love made visible. And if you cannot
work with love but only with distaste, it is
better that you should leave your work..."
KAHLIL GIBRAN, WRITER

f you think that Job One is creating your résumé, you've jumped
a step. The first task for any job seeker is to determine what
kind of job you should be seeking. While for some this step
may seem obvious, understanding your abilities and passions is a
critical first step. Many people simply focus on what's available,
but remember that job postings are often written by Human
Resources (HR) departments, and may be generic. When you
are clear on the kind of job you are best suited for, you can make
a far more powerful presentation of your abilities both in the
interview and in your résumé.

Surprisingly, most people have more clarity on what they
don't want to do than what they do want, yet achieving clarity

is critical for success, not just in the application process but also on the job.

Alyssa finally landed a position writing code for a gaming software company. Excited by the prospect (and the envy of her friends), Alyssa couldn't wait to start. The New York-based company had only a small physical presence, so most of the employees had to work from home. Though a social person, Alyssa relished the prospect of avoiding both a long commute and the cost of nice business attire. She couldn't wait to apply her skills to the job. As with most development jobs, her first assignment was to perform basic maintenance work on existing programs, not new development. She found the detailed and exacting work boring and the lack of in-person, team interaction frustrating. Most programmers simply put their heads down and get the work done. She never realized how much she enjoyed the camaraderie of an office, nor had she understood that her passion for programming had been in creating new games, not patching existing ones. At the three-month mark, Alyssa found herself seriously considering looking for another job.

When she had begun applying for jobs, Alyssa knew she didn't want one that required a long commute, though there were some aspects of onsite jobs that she liked. Google's offering of three gourmet meals a day, access to a well-designed gym and all the other benefits of some of the Silicon Valley companies appealed to her, but Google never called. As to the specifics of the job, she had never really considered that there might be different types of coding. In college, maintenance coding wasn't required. Everything she coded, often with a team of other students, was new work. Her passion was creation, but she hadn't really asked what the job would entail.

Do you know what the job of your dreams looks like? If you don't clearly understand what you excel at and what you love to do, you can't answer the question. In fact, most people know precisely what they don't like and don't enjoy. We could make lists of these things. But when asked what you love to do, many find themselves stumped. It isn't simply the opposite of what you don't want. That would be too easy.

As it turns out, we all have a lot of things we are good at or could become good at. Tests have evolved to help you match these up with actual jobs. You probably had the chance to take some of these at school. But one thing is missing from these assessments. No one asks you what you would like to do. Of the list of things you are great at, the number of items you actually enjoy is much smaller. From this more manageable list, you can more easily figure out what you should be doing. If you also align this list with your values, you can discover where you can offer something unique and special to the world; you can create a life of meaning out of this formula. More importantly, the passion you connect to when you find these areas makes you stand out in interviews. In a tight job market, companies can afford to wait to find the right candidate, the one who is personally driven to excel in the job.

When you were a child, you instinctively understood the importance of doing what you love and what you're good at. Expectations and training tend to drive that out of our thought processes. We joke about 'work' being a four-letter word. That doesn't spell passion and enthusiasm. Even though people might think it should be obvious to connect with our joy, getting clarity takes some work, but this is fun work. What's better than figuring out how great you are and how much fun you can have? I call this finding your 'Happiness Intersection.'

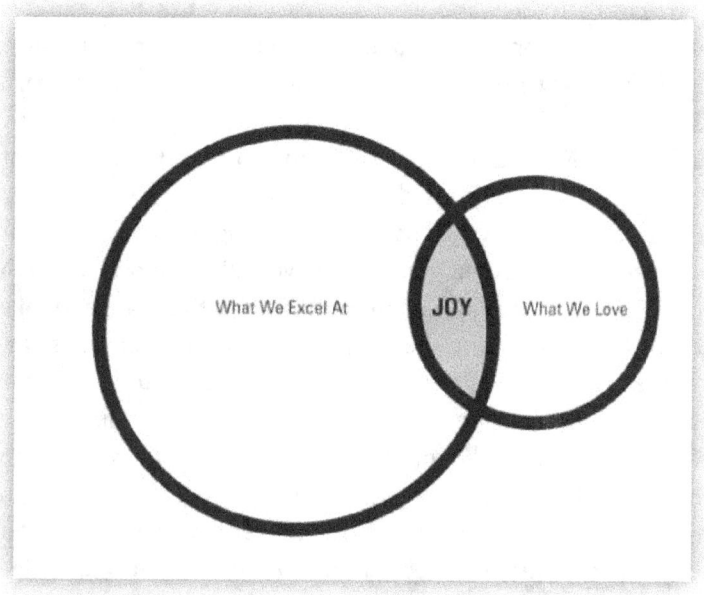

Figure 1 - The Happiness Intersection Point

But how do you get there? First, you have to figure out what you excel at—what you do really well.

Exercise 1-1 – On a sheet of paper (or your screen), write "Things I Am Great At." Over the next week or so, add items to this list as you think of them. Don't limit yourself to items that seem like they would fit in with a career. Note everything.

Also, be detailed. Don't say simply 'accounting.' Describe the parts of accounting that you excel in, such as balancing accounts, keeping records, or producing reports. If possible, describe the circumstances where you excel, such as 'working with a group' or 'outdoors.' You might feel that you do best when there is a clearly defined leader, or where you have short assignments with frequent wins. Consider these aspects as well as the types of things you are great at.

It can also be useful to look at other areas of your life for inspiration and ideas.

- Volunteer work
- Hobbies
- What you did well as a child
- What you have taken classes in and enjoyed, even if you never used the skill
- What you do as chores, such as gardening or cleaning
- Movies, books, music and games you like
- Sports, clubs you belong to, and other social activities.

If your list isn't long, ask friends and family. Sometimes, it can be hard to see yourself as others see you. Take as much time as you need to get a complete list. Even trivial items can be informative.

Most people excel at quite a few things, so keep at it until you have at least 20 items.

Exercise 1-2 – When the list is complete, go back and circle every item that you still love to do. Most likely, the list will be much shorter now. Few people love everything they are good at. Create a new list titled 'What I Love to Do and Excel At.' These represent your 'Happiness Intersection' and will help you formulate a career that makes sense.

Vikram found his MBA helped him land a job working for a large CPA firm. Quick with numbers and highly disciplined, he felt this would be a good match. However, the job he was given was auditing the various clients, a job involving travel, strange working conditions and engaging with many groups of people. Though he was competent at all of it, he found himself dreading the next trip, the next audit. His dream of work involved workdays in an office, with occasional meetings with colleagues, no travel and a lot less client interaction. He felt best running numbers at his desk quietly, with limited interruptions. Instead, he found himself one week at a winery, trying to log data while leaning against a rack of wine barrels, the next week coughing dust at a lumber yard. Clients constantly interrupted him, sometimes with useful information, but mostly to make sure he had the data they wanted to provide. Vikram had found the perfect job for his capabilities, but one that was a poor match for what he loved.

Sometimes, we get stuck on deciding what it would look like to love the work you do. For this, it can be helpful to remember when we felt the way a perfect job should feel. Positive psychologist Mihaly Csikszentmihaly defined the term 'flow' to mean "being completely involved in an activity for its own sake. The ego falls away. Time flies. Every action, movement, and thought follows inevitably from the previous one, like playing jazz. Your whole being is involved, and you're using your skills to the utmost."[1]   When 'flow' happens, you feel as if you are simply absorbed in the activity and the work completes itself. While no one spends every moment of work in this state, when you find work you love and excel at, you will find yourself experiencing more moments like this.

By understanding what you are good at AND love, you ensure that your search will be more likely to result in a great job 'fit.' Very few skills inventories or other assessment tools provide you with the same kind of information. You may have had the chance to try some of these, but in some cases the results seemed to make no sense. I learned that I would be a great spy, music teacher or naval officer. None of these appealed at the time, and while an in-depth study might have revealed the skills that led to these 'suggestions,' taking that approach wouldn't have been the right move for me.

Exercise 1-3 – With the list you created in Exercise 1-2 in front of you, spend time each day reading the various items out loud. Think about them. When one seems interesting, write more about that item. What details can you provide about what got that item on that list? What do you feel when you do this activity? Under what situations would you enjoy doing this? By getting more detail on these items, you begin to construct what a work day might look like to you. In some cases, the item, though accurate, represents something broader, something more attainable. An example can be helpful.

Desiree reviewed the list she had created, wondering what she would do with such items as 'work with animals,' 'play with my old toys,' 'create craft projects,' and 'coach sports.'

---

1   Geirland, John, "Go With The Flow," Wired, 1996, http://archive.wired.com/wired/archive/4.09/czik_pr.html

While some of the items could lead to jobs, the idea of training to be a sports coach, or competing with thousands for the few animal trainer jobs available, just didn't sound right. When she asked herself what that would look like, she imagined herself spending days trying to keep small animals, particularly cats, entertained. While that sounded like it might lead to setting up a pet-sitting service or a hotel for cats, she looked deeper. Why cats? What made that work for her?

She realized that she respected cats more than other animals because they discriminated and chose those they would sit with. She liked the way a cat would develop when confronted with challenges and stimulation, just like a young child. In fact, she had taken most of the classes required to enter a teacher credentialing program, but hadn't really considered it because it just seemed like one of a narrow band of obvious career choices. And yet, as she considered it more carefully, she found she really liked the idea of working in a school, particularly some of the newer, experimental charter schools. The more she tossed the idea around in her head, the more it resonated. And working with younger children would allow her to coach, play with toys and create ideas for fun art projects. Desiree couldn't wait to get started.

As Desiree found, you can do this work by yourself, taking the time to really ponder and consider each of the items in the list you created. Alternatively, you may find that a coach or trusted advisor can help you sort through ideas faster, pose questions and challenge assumptions. The more people you share your ideas with, the more input you will receive on types of jobs that might match the intersection points you have identified. After all, none of us really know all the job possibilities out there. And few of us, even after happy and successful careers, would say that we had worked in the areas we thought we would when we were children. Open your mind to the possibilities.

"If you want to envision a happy person's stance, imagine one foot rooted in the present with mindful appreciation of what one has — and another foot reaching toward the future for yet-to-be-uncovered sources of meaning."
Robert Biswas-Diener and Todd B. Kashdan, psychologists

Summary

Only when you find the intersection of what you love to do and what you're good at will you find a career that will truly make you happy and successful. It's worth the upfront effort to figure this out; it's too easy to end up in a career devoid of meaning. Most of us feel an imperative to do something that matters. Your Happiness Intersection will show you where you can make the most difference in the world.

CHAPTER 2

Working the 'Secret'

"Thoughts become things."
MIKE DOOLEY, WRITER

In 2006, a DVD called 'The Secret' began exciting a lot of people with the idea of 'the law of attraction', which says that what you think about most is what you attract into your life. Followed shortly by a book, many got excited about the idea that all they had to do was think about something and they would have it. A transforming moment showed a girl admiring a necklace; by thinking about owning it, she ended up with the necklace. This example drew an audience, but the compelling and well-documented power of thought was better shown in other examples, such as the badly injured pilot who visualized walking again by Christmas when no one believed he would ever walk again.

In fact, the 'law of attraction' isn't a genie who will produce valuables at your command. Instead, it has to do with clarity, communication, consciousness and commitment. We will discuss the four "c's" in this chapter.

Clarity is what the exercises in Chapter 1 were designed to help you achieve. When you are clear and specific on a goal, you are much more likely to achieve it. Next, you want to communicate your goal to others, even those you don't know well. The answers and opportunities are out there, but you need to make sure others know about your ideas.

Consciousness means that when you have clarity, you also need to be conscious of external realities and choices. This is how you make your 'luck.' You may dream of being an astronaut, but if even if you're good at science or a remarkable pilot, you probably won't achieve that goal. When one market is flooded with applicants, it can be prudent to look at a different market, especially one with more opportunities.

People who communicate their dreams and plans tend to find out about job openings, internships, training opportunities and even volunteer work which could lead to a job. Finally, commitment means understanding that it takes time, and that you need to persevere.

Henry Ford said it, in his own way: "If you think you can or you think you can't, you're right." Or as coaches put it: you get more of what you pay attention to. That's it–that's "the secret." These observations offer empowerment to anyone seeking to find their Happiness Intersection, whether it is in the workplace or any other aspect of their lives.

Sometimes, we can feel a little lacking in self-esteem. After working through your list in the last chapter, check in with friends and family. Let them validate your excellence. Become grounded in the reality of what you are great at.

When successful people are asked why they triumphed when so many others failed, many will note that their secret was simply that they believed they could do it. "Can't" wasn't in their vocabulary, and it shouldn't be in yours. The job market may be tough, but unless there are no jobs, there is a great job out there for you. Successful people didn't build their business overnight or get their dream job the first time out there. Dry spells, frustrations and delays are part of life. But the heroes of the business world were clear on one thing – they saw themselves as already successful. They had already made it even as they were learning, building up their résumé and moving up the ladder.

Eliana struggled to get through community college. The first in her family to make it past high school, she felt pressure to achieve more than her older brothers and her parents, all of whom had jobs she considered menial. Her mother in particular pushed her. "Ellie," she said. "I don't want you to ever have to wash dishes for a living. I want more for you."

In her junior year, a favorite teacher pulled her aside and asked her why she wasn't taking a more challenging class. "I can barely handle what I have," Eliana told her. "No one in my family could do this. I'm doing better than they did, even if I only get some college credits."

"Not good enough," the teacher said, smiling. "I know what you can do. I see you reaching out for that diploma, looking out at the horizon, and envisioning the next step on your career." Moved, Eliana found herself seeing that vision, too. She remembered how much something like that had helped to get through a long hike once. A friend described how they would feel at the end of the hike, the cold water they would sip from the fountain, and what the vista would be at the top. The vision spurred her to walk faster and with more energy. Perhaps that kind of vision could get her through the next two years.

There are two sides to every picture. 'The Secret' can also impact you in another way: creating what appears to be a run of back luck. When everyone else is finding a job, you can't. You have too many unpaid bills, and when times are tough, bad things just seem to start happening to you. When you find yourself experiencing a lot of negative events, it's natural to focus on the negative. But the problem is that this focus on negativity tends to bring in more negativity. Even when a great opportunity presents itself, the negative mind-trap you're in can transform your impression of the event. In reality, we make our own luck by noticing positives and then focusing on them.

Sanjay struggled after he left college. First, he had a hard time finding a place he could afford; then, shortly after he moved, his apartment was robbed. Depressed, he found each day offered him more conviction that he was doomed. Then, his friend, Gupta, suggested that he look at the things he had instead of what he lacked. Sanjay became angry at the suggestion and railed at Gupta. "When you've tried everything else, consider my idea." Gupta said.

Sanjay considered his friend the happiest person he knew, so he had to think about it. The next day, he started the morning by listing the good things in his life, noting the great job he had landed, while others were stuck in jobs well below their potential. He liked his neighborhood, even after the robbery. Once the landlord changed the locks and reinforced the door, he felt safe there. Each morning, he walked to work through a park, enjoying the sight of people walking a variety of pets. The next day, he found himself in front of an SPCA shelter near his office and went home with a mixed-breed spaniel of his own. Walks with his dog, Fancy, helped him explore even more of his wonderful surroundings. A bit disgruntled, he had to admit that once he focused on the positive, his life seemed transformed. And even the normal, disagreeable aspects of his life no longer seemed so awful.

Where do you stand in the luck lottery? Are you in control of your fate?
Exercise 2-1 – Ask yourself these questions:

1. Do you see yourself as lucky?
2. Do you face challenges confidently, sure that you'll prevail?
3. Do you rate yourself as having high self-esteem?

If not, you may wish to start. Try this exercise:
Exercise 2-2

1. At the end of each day, write down five good things about the day
2. Once a week, write down the three (positive) adjectives that best describe you
3. When something bad happens, take a deep breath and ask yourself what good could come of it, even if it is only that you might laugh about this down the road or that you survived.

For many, changing the way you think can be a little challenging, but the value of doing so is great. In Star Wars, Yoda says "Do or do not. There is no try." As you go through the book, there will be many opportunities to experiment with new approaches or ways of thinking. But in the end, only those things you commit to will happen. When you set out to succeed and visualize the success, you are already halfway to achieving it. This is all about the first 'c,' clarity. This is 'the Secret.'

The second 'c' is communication. When you tell people what you plan to do, you make the commitment real. But communication has a secondary and even more powerful effect. When you tell people something, you find yourself tapping into solutions. The next job, the next opportunity may simply be the luck of who sits next to you on public transit, if only you let him or her know what you are trying to do. When you put a question out to the universe, answers appear as if by magic. Then you have to be willing to do whatever it takes.

Jeanette boarded the plane, looking forward to a brief respite from looking for work. She would be spending the long weekend with her parents at their Wisconsin summer home. As she settled in for the ride, she noticed the tag on her seatmate's briefcase. If she could land her dream job at her dream company, it would have been the company he worked for. They began to chat, as seatmates do, and she asked him about how he liked his company. William, a senior sales representative, spoke passionately about the company. He asked her what she did and she described the kind of work she wanted to do. "I'm just out of college, but I've had some summer intern experience at software companies," she said. Smiling shyly, she confessed, "Your company is at the top of my list. Do you think they might be interested in me?"

"We're always looking for good candidates," William said. "Here's my card. Send me your résumé and a few job postings that look good to you and I'll see what I can do."

Jeanette had no contacts in her network and one had just dropped into her lap. She made a point of following up with William as soon as she could get to her tablet and search the company's job listings.

No one can help you if they don't know you need help. But note that Jeanette didn't rush into the 'ask.' Instead, she got to know him, showed interest in him and let the conversation naturally flow to her area of interest. People like to help people they like.

The third 'c' is 'consciousness'. Once you have identified the path you wish to take, you have to do the work of figuring out how you could realize your goal. If you simply ask people, "Do you have a job at your company? ", even the most helpful will be somewhat put off. You haven't done the work. Look at job listings, talk to people about the kinds of work they do, keep learning. Check the Internet for market pricing so you can understand the reality of what jobs pay.

The final 'c' is commitment. You have to be fully committed to doing this. It will take work. Good things don't always happen overnight. But when you are clear on your purpose, communicate it, and do the homework, you will get the payoff. Visualize yourself already there, while taking steps to make it possible. Describe yourself in that role. Visualization is very powerful because, until you can actually imagine yourself in that role, it can be hard to see the steps needed to get there.

"Your imagination is your preview of life's coming attractions."

The Secret" is real, but it isn't much of a secret. As you can see, it isn't as simple as rubbing a lamp and making a wish. It takes work. Yet nothing is more worthwhile, or more rewarding than achieving a goal you care deeply about.

"You see, idealism detached from action is just a dream. But idealism allied with pragmatism, with rolling up your sleeves and making the world bend a bit, is very exciting. It's very real. It's very strong."
– Bono, singer

Summary

To achieve your dreams, you must be crystal clear on what they are. Too often, we start down a road hoping it will take us where we want to go without a clear understanding of where that might be. When you take the time to really understand yourself and what the right job is for you now, you have a far greater chance of achieving it. Trust in yourself, not in hope.

CHAPTER 3

Define Opportunities

"Seek not to change the world, but choose
to change your mind about the world."
— A Course in Miracles

You now have some idea of what you'd love to do, but the next part is to translate that into a job. For those who went to college or a technical school, you may have started with a clear vision of your career path. However, as you went through your program, feelings and interests might have changed. In addition, none of us really knows all the ways a set of skills can be employed. We know the obvious ones, but the real job gems are those you didn't even know existed. And of course, for some, the field that was red-hot when they began either no longer exists or the available job market has shrunk.

Even if you have a pretty good idea of what you want to do, it's always useful to get some additional information about the possibilities. You can take a variety of career inventory tests, which can also point to specific types of jobs. To find these, many of which are free, Google 'career aptitude tests.' You'll find many options. It can be useful to try more than one, as the results vary. If you are still associated with a school, many have career departments that can offer these tests as well. With the understanding you gained in Chapter 1, the output of such tests helps you understand the test output and to make it useful to you. There are online 'skills profilers' which can help you as well. A few sample sites will be listed in the Resources section, with the caveat that these sites can come and go. You can always search them out by typing in the same keywords I used. Another option is to Google some of the keywords you came up with. Type in 'job' and add a list of things you love and want to do.

Madison studied math in college. For the first two years, she felt the same passion she had in high school, where algebra and geometry came easily to her. She used her skill to trounce her friends when they played poker. Numbers were her friend.

Then, everything changed. The numbers went away and theory and proofs became the name of the game, a game she no longer enjoyed playing. She could do the work; it just wasn't work she wanted to do. Madison had secretly dreamed of being a math professor focused on helping other women succeed in this male-dominated profession. Now, she didn't know where to go. Pressed by her parents, she finished out with a business degree, a piece of paper that meant nothing to her. *When I'm so good at this, shouldn't I find a way to do it?* A few people suggested accounting, but though she had sailed through the classes, she knew she would slit her wrists if she had to sit in an office and crunch budget numbers all day. Still, it was a well-paying job.

Finally, in desperation, she went to her college's career office and took some tests. She also browsed the various job descriptions. A counselor suggested she search on a combination of math and gambling, since she had shared her enjoyment of beating the odds. It turned out that there were all kinds of interesting opportunities in the stock market where a gift for numbers and an appetite for risk translated to great jobs.

Another important step is to put your interest out there to anyone who will listen. Tell everyone that you are really good at the skills and abilities you have identified. Let them suggest ideas. The interesting thing is that, where you might see a wall too high to scale, someone else might have a 'ladder' or a 'door' into that desired end. Answers to the most challenging problems we face are out there. We simply have to let people know we're asking. Even strangers can be an amazing resource.

Rihanna barely eked her way through college, working two jobs and taking fewer classes than she would have liked to. First in her family to go to college, she couldn't ask her parents to work even longer hours to help with her expenses. Her mother's hands were coarse and red from the long hours of cleaning other people's houses. Rihanna wanted to find a way to do well enough so she could pay her parents back for their sacrifices. But she didn't want to work like that. She studied psychology as an undergraduate, desiring someday to have a practice of her own. But she needed grad school, a cost she couldn't manage. She had to work as much as possible and it was hard to manage daily college around her jobs.

One day, on the bus to school, she sat next to an older woman. The woman had her head down, focused on her tablet, working hard on something. Finally, she looked up.

"Homework," she said. "I'm doing an online degree in psych."

"Really?" Rihanna had never heard of such a thing.

"Only way it would work for me," the woman said. "I'm on the road for work all the time. Couldn't attend a physical school if my life depended on it. It's tough — you have to be pretty disciplined. But it works for me."

Delighted, Rihanna copied down the name of the college, an accredited institution that also offered online degrees. Even better, they weren't as expensive as the places she considered before.

There is a kind of synchronicity to the world. When you put out a question, you often find you get an answer. Ask it of everyone and anyone, and you get a wider variety of answers. Ask anyone in their 40s or 50s: the vast majority of them are not doing the job they dreamed of when they were younger, but they are generally doing something they enjoy and care about. The challenge is to become aware of all the various possibilities, then not rule out any area until you have more thoroughly explored it. While many think in terms of corporations they might work for, other options may not be as obvious.

Charitable organizations employ people as well as relying on volunteers. Often, the most interesting jobs available only go to full-time employees. Government, at all levels, hires people, often in jobs that only exist in that sector. Someone in love with nature might look at jobs in landscape architecture, but jobs with organizations such as the Sierra Club or government agencies, such as the National Forest Service, are also viable options. The military offers an appealing proposition to those who can't afford the training they need. Military 'hires' can get valuable training and experience, which allows you to launch a successful non-military career, leapfrogging past those who have only education, but not experience. Another option, more feasible and achievable in the Internet age, is self-employment. Where it once could be a huge cost and challenge to initiate a business, people of all ages are creating small businesses and driving their own agendas.

At early stages of a job search, the most important factor is to discover as many options as you can. Create a huge list then winnow it down to the best options for you. Until you know all the possibilities, you shouldn't go too far in your job hunt. A good analogy is whether you would rather do your grocery shopping at the local 7-11 or at a major chain, such as Safeway. Most people prefer a store that provides them with choice. It works for jobs, too. Don't get stuck on details at this point. Salary and benefits are issues you consider when you begin to winnow down the options, not in creating your option list.

An interesting point comes when we assume we know a field really well. While you might not fall into this trap, many do. I'm a perfect example of this. As soon as I learned how to write, I wanted to be a writer, but received discouragement from adults who felt that the field was simply too risky. For every Stephen King or John Grisham, there are thousands of people who never publish or who publish but can't live on their earnings. Still, I couldn't 'not' write, so I continued to create work and send it out. As predicted, I never made enough to live on. But while I was engaged in what my mother might have deemed a futile effort, I was learning my craft and putting in the 10,000 hours required to gain mastery.

As my real world career progressed, I noticed that many people in IT couldn't write. And yet, writing opportunities abounded. Though many assignments didn't offer scope for creativity, others did, and what I discovered was that ALL writing helped me become better. None of my jobs included the title 'writer', yet that is exactly what I was doing, full-time, and with a better paycheck than I ever earned submitting to newspapers and magazines. I also could write what I wanted when I wasn't working on corporate writing. Without realizing the possibilities, I lucked into doing exactly what I wanted.

Don't get held back by titles or job descriptions. What you want to do for the next few years may not be rewarded with the title of your dreams, but it might be the job you truly want. Only when you are clear on what you want can you match that with the many ways that job can manifest itself in the real world.

While building towards a career is a laudable goal, remember that many will have multiple careers in a lifetime. That gives us the freedom to do something passionately and fully for a few years, knowing that we have a chance to change our course when we feel ready. The process that you are going through now becomes easier as you learn how to assess yourself and find the jobs that match your current expertise and interests. Sometimes it helps to realize that you aren't picking the last job you'll ever love, just the next one.

Don't you ever let a soul in the world tell you that you can't be exactly who you are."
– Lady Gaga, singer

Summary

Before you apply for a job, take the time to match your skills, expertise and interests to real jobs. The most obvious use of your talents might not be the best fit, so consider all the ways in which your abilities can make you successful. Talk to people, get input, and ask people what they like about their jobs. A great job may be the one you never considered.

CHAPTER 4

Résumé Preparation

"People are always blaming their
circumstances for what they are. I
don't believe in circumstances."
— GEORGE BERNARD SHAW, WRITER

A résumé is still required for career jobs. Since you don't have to use a typewriter to create these anymore, there's no reason not to create one for each position. You begin with a master résumé and adapt it to match the particulars of the job. Why do this? Each position requires slightly different skills as well as interests. You want to focus attention on the match between your experience and their requirements.

Elizar spent a weekend crafting what he thought was a great résumé. Friends and his family agreed. He had taken summer and after-school jobs and made it seem as if he had enough experience to apply for the entry level management position he sought. With the help of his college placement officer, he found a few companies offering such positions and mailed off his résumé with a carefully-worded cover letter.

He had created the résumé before he began looking at jobs, using generic language. Most of the time, he focused on thinking about how exciting it would be to start at one of these places. He didn't notice the wording of the job posting, nor did his résumé specifically focus on what they requested. After a few weeks, Elizar felt discouraged; he had heard nothing from any of the companies. A fellow management student told him that he had landed a position with one of the same companies where Elizar had applied. What had his friend done differently? Why hadn't he even scored an interview?

The small amount of time it takes to tailor and print a fresh résumé for each position pays off in interviews and call-backs. Create a folder for your versions, with one file entitled 'Master Résumé.' Label each file in a way that helps you and the employer keep track of the document.

Ex. Res-dpkalm-Schwab-10-15. This file-name tells them the date of my submission as well as my name. The company name is to help you distinguish one file from another. It's a simple step, but one that is appreciated when a company needs to save a copy of your document.

Before talking about how to tailor the résumé, the first concern is format. In some cases, there is a standard they ask you to use, but in most situations, it's up to you. If you want to make the investment, select a current (no more than one-year-old) guide. Most libraries maintain a nice selection of job reference guides, so you can save yourself money, as well as consider a variety of possibilities. In some industries, such as IT, the format is somewhat dictated by the skills they want to see. You may find a request to list all programming languages or operating systems you know.

While there are many job hunting sites with similar information, the first that showed up on a recent Google search was a guide by Monster: http://career-advice.monster.com/resumes-cover-letters/resume-samples/sample-resumes-by-industry/article.aspx. It's easy to find examples online and select one that allows you to best highlight your accomplishments. Some are specifically designed for people with less experience. Take the time to review several sites and more than one book before you select a style.

You always want to lead with a clear objective. If applying to a job with a title, the objective is not that title. As an example, if you are looking for a marketing intern position, your objective might be "a position that leverages my experience while helping me learn the social media, writing and other communications skills essential to fulfill a senior role." Where possible, use words from the job description in your résumé. Sadly, given the capabilities of computers these days, many human resources departments begin by running the paperwork through a program that seeks out the key words. Don't let yourself be eliminated that easily.

Next up is how to describe your experience. It's critical to put yourself in the hiring manager's seat as you complete this section. For some, much of your experience might be in part-time service jobs. This is where the real work of résumé writing begins. You want to translate what you did into what you can do for someone else. For customer-facing jobs, ask:

- Did I solve key problems for customers? How did I do this?
- Did I find a more efficient way to do my job?
- Have I saved the company money or, by my direct actions, caused them to make more money?
- What was the impact of my position on the company's bottom line?

This kind of analysis can be challenging, so get some help. Ask people already in the market to review what you wrote, or even hire a résumé coach to see how it can be made stronger. What you want to do is transform "McDonald's Order Taker – worked part-time at McDonald's at the register and also making fries' to "Customer Service, McDonald's – Consistently upsold customers to larger orders and to featured products; quickly resolved any customer complaints which resulted in increases in repeat business; focused my work on delighting customers every day so McDonald's became their fast-food choice." Which person would you rather hire?

Another critical factor is to put your most important qualities first. Though many companies prefer a chronological listing, you can select another approach, if that better serves to promote you. Headers such as 'Core Competencies' and 'Proven Results' allow you to show specific instances of your value, as well as highlighting that you understand what the company is looking for. Don't forget to include significant volunteer experiences. Again, you want to look for what you learned and delivered that will help make you more successful on the job. It often happens that the fast food clerk by day has spent summers working on something such as Habitat for Humanity and has learned how to: ". . . work effectively on constantly changing teams, pick up skills readily after a short training, measure and cut accurately, complete a project", etc. As you develop more real career experience, some of these entries will naturally be eliminated from your résumé. It is a constantly evolving document which should be assessed every year, even if you aren't looking for a job.

Use action words: accomplished, created, saved, led, etc. Avoid words such as 'assisted' or 'helped.' Though your contribution might have been as a member of a team, these words diminish the effort. Another key point of note: use a professional email address, even if you have to create one simply for this purpose. Gmail is great for this. It should sound professional and clearly relate to you. If you can get it, the best bet is your initials & last-name@email server.com. Give several ways to reach you – phone, cell phone and address.

Keep the résumé to two pages or less. In reality, the more you include, the less they will read. You can use a few 'cheats' such as smaller margins and a smaller font, but don't go smaller than 11 point. Some of your hiring managers have aging eyes and, if they have to work to read it, they won't.

The résumé guides will help you lay out your competencies in a clear manner, but they don't always emphasize that, for print résumés, you want high-quality paper. It's worth the investment to buy 22-24 lb. paper of a neutral shade or white. And though it should go without saying, you will ideally present the résumé unfolded. Carry copies to interviews in a folder to keep them clean and pristine. If you have to mail it, fold it in thirds and use a standard No. 10 envelope.

After you have your master résumé drafted, show it to friends, family, and people you know who already have jobs like the one you want. Get their input. Some of us can be a little too modest or use less-than powerful words to describe our capabilities. Impartial eyes can find these problems and help you correct them.

Sound like a lot of work? It doesn't have to be, if you have a good plan. Reviewing style guides and formats might take a few hours. Once you have selected your format, most people find they can complete a great master over a weekend. Add a few days to get it reviewed and edited and you should be able to have your master ready in less than a week. Adapting it to each position you apply for shouldn't take more than an hour.

Part of the preparation is the creation of the cover letter. Typically, formats for these are included in all résumé guides. The purpose is to highlight what makes you the right candidate for this particular job and to show your interest in the position. It is also a place to include information that didn't make sense in a résumé. This letter should be reviewed carefully with friends and family as well. It should be no more than three paragraphs and be given with each résumé copy. If you are interviewing, bring several copies of each. Bring lots of copies of your master résumé to a career fair. And it never hurts to always have a copy with you. When you talk to people on public transit, at a sporting event or a lecture, you never know when a casual conversation will turn serious. This brings up the final point in résumé preparation – the elevator pitch.

Once you know (from working the previous chapters) what you want to do, you will need to develop a short 'pitch' defining the goal in terms that address the needs of the person you are speaking with. It isn't a complete recitation of your résumé; it's designed to spark interest and lead to further conversation.

> Joaquin had quickly learned that there weren't a lot of posted positions for his skill set, but he had been told by his career advisor at school that the jobs were out there. "The challenge is that these jobs don't get listed," his advisor said. "You have to know someone." Initially daunted at the challenge, Joaquin decided that even if he didn't know hiring managers, he might be able to interest fellow techies at local conferences and meetings. He got his résumé in order, wrote a cover letter and worked on creating a short pitch. He planned to refine it as he talked to people. He also memorized it, so that he could recite it easily no matter where he found himself.
>
> His pitch was simple. When asked about what he was doing, he said, "I'm looking for a position that will allow me to help people make the best use of the software they have purchased. As the resident 'techie' in my family, I have helped both family and friends successfully navigate new systems, solve problems and become power users. I have a passion for empowering people to enjoy technology and get optimal use from it."

It didn't take long before Joaquin found someone working in support at a major software company who very much wanted his company to hire more help. His clear statement showed not only his capabilities but also his desire to serve. Understand that it will take time to craft such a cogent and well-worded statement and that you may have to adapt it over time.

"I didn't have time to write a short letter, so I wrote a long one instead."
– Mark Twain, writer

QUICK TIP 1: If asked to email a résumé, don't email it as an attachment unless specifically asked to do so. Copy and paste it into your email. Many people are either worried about or forbidden to download external documents which may contain computer viruses. Check how it looks before sending. Some typestyles don't copy and paste well. Correct any 'wrap-arounds'; email programs often truncate lines at 72 characters, so some of your content might be pushed to a separate line.

QUICK TIP 2: Believe your résumé. Gain confidence in the skills you already have, your native intelligence, and your ability to work hard. If you don't believe in yourself, no one else will. But if you can connect with your passion and your abilities, other people will be drawn to you and see the value of giving you a job.

Summary
Take your time to create a quality résumé which reflects an understanding of the job. Tailor your résumé and cover letter to the specific position. In an online world, your résumé is your face in the world. Make it great.

CHAPTER 5

Social Presence

> "Sometimes you can't see yourself clearly until
> you see yourself through the eyes of others."
> — ELLEN DEGENERES, ENTERTAINER

By the time you begin to look for a career position, you will most likely have a substantial social presence, meaning that you have accounts on various social networks and probably appear in pictures or videos shot by others. While in school, updates on Facebook and Pinterest serve to keep us all connected, making us part of our friends' lives. It's fun and appealing. It's also dangerous.

Selena knew she had spent too many hours on social sites, updating her status and sending out tweets. Once she graduated, she resolved to watch how much time she invested in keeping track of people she knew. A career counselor had told her to focus on getting her LinkedIn network going and creating a dynamic profile. She had spent some time on that, but found herself sneaking over to see what people were doing and who had 'tagged' her in pictures. Connecting this way felt like attending an endless party where you never knew who would come through the 'front door' with an interesting update.

One day, a favorite aunt asked to friend her and she agreed. Aunt Becca called her the next day. "Dear, have you seen all the pictures of you? Some of them are . . . well, not that nice."

Selena logged on and together they scanned the photos of parties and events. At first, Selena found the pictures a reminder of great times, but through the eyes of her aunt, she became uncomfortable with the images. "But only my friends can see them," she said.

"That's not true," Becca said. "I saw them before you friended me. That's part of why I asked. I wanted to see what was visible before and after."

Selena hadn't known nor had she thought to check. She wondered how easy it would be for a prospective employer to see her at her worst. *Could it keep me from getting hired?*

The simple answer is 'yes.' Employers always look at your social image before making a hiring decision. In some cases, the scan may happen early in the process, just to thin the stack of applications and résumés. Later in the process, some employers may ask for your password, demand that you friend them or simply ask you to login so they can browse various sites. While you can't stop the ever-present cell phone cameras from capturing you, you can ask that friends not tag you, or even to take down the picture. You can also be more aware of your behavior when in

the presence of others. A good approach is to create cell-phone-free zones at parties where no one is allowed to take pictures.

That may help the picture problem, but what about your words? In general, if you know that people are looking, it can be useful to have a social media 'handle,' an alternate name that isn't easily connected to you. You might use your name for one Twitter feed–the harmless, intelligent, sharing one–while creating an alter-ego if you wish to share opinions. Go back and look at your profiles and comments as if you were evaluating someone you didn't know for a job. How would they see you? No one expects that every interaction on the Web will be professional, but you want the general impression to be positive.

But you never know what other people are saying about you. Or do you? Google provides Google Alerts, a valuable, free resource which allows you to create multiple alerts based on the various ways your name might appear. You want to cover them all:

- First name, last name
- First name, middle initial, last name
- First name, middle name, last name

Set up the alerts to send you a list of what they find on whatever frequency you prefer. A weekly update is probably sufficient for most. When you find out where you appear, you have a chance to correct it, or, at least to be prepared to respond to it. Just to start, type your name into the Search bar and see what happens. While only ten years ago you might have found nothing, most people now have an extensive list.

In a later chapter, I'll talk about creating a personal brand and how to use it to create a good web presence. I'll also talk about how to make LinkedIn work for you. But for now, consider your social presence the way your Aunt Becca might. Who do you want to be? This is your chance to manage the message, to create the person online you want to be.

> "O would some power the giftie gie us to see ourselves as others see us.
> (O would some power the gift to give us to see ourselves as others see us.)"
> **Robert Burns**, poet

Summary

With the many social and photo sites out there, anyone can find out more about you than ever before. Be proactive and manage the image you project online. Google yourself and discover what employers will quickly find. Manage your privacy settings carefully.

CHAPTER 6

Building a Network

"All men are caught in an inescapable
network of mutuality."
DR. MARTIN LUTHER KING, JR., HUMANITARIAN

veryone knows they need to network, but it may seem really hard to get out there and do it. If you've been to a networking event, you may find yourself questioning the value of spending your time in that way, as one after another person approaches you trying to score a 'win.' Networking isn't simply about getting a long list of people who agree to 'friend' you or be LinkedIn with you, though there is value in growing your list. What matters is who is on that list. At first, you might begin by wanting to add people who can help you and some of those will be willing to connect with you. But in many cases, it can work out better to think about networking requests from the perspective of the person you are asking. Just remember–a powerful network is probably the best way to land a job. Now, it

is more about who you know than what you know, at least to get your foot in the door.

Maclain had just begun a job selling car insurance, but he was a contractor, paid only for the sales he made. Knowing this, he tried to convert every contact into a contract, but so far, this hadn't worked for him. At a speed networking event, he handed his card to each person he met, telling them how he could save them money on insurance. What could be more compelling than that?

Attending a weekly networking lunch, he couldn't wait to make his pitch in front of the group. After the meeting, one of the members approached him and said, "Maclain, I have to ask you. How's your approach working for you?"

Maclain looked at his feet. "Not so hot," he said. "And I don't get it. I have great prices and plans to offer. I can't even get people to give me a card. Who knows what we could do together, if I only had the chance?"

The member smiled at Maclain. "I thought like you when I started out, too. But networking involves two elements you're missing. First, you don't seem interested in the other person. You're leading with your need – the need to close a deal. Second, you're rushing things. Sometimes, the best way to get ahead is to start with curiosity about the other person. Then, you find out if they even have a need."

The standard sales funnel comes in handy here. You start by getting to know a person well enough that they will be willing to talk to you about their needs. Next, you establish if they have

a need that you could fill. If so, is it compelling enough to cause them to take action?

- Connect
- Compel
- Close

How does that translate to in-person networking? Of course, you have your card ready to hand out. But rather than leading with information about you and your need (a job), what would happen if you asked them about themselves? When you show interest in a person and truly listen to them without inserting your own agenda, you offer them a gift beyond price. It's rare to feel truly heard. 'Connecting' is all about learning about each other; lead with questions and give someone the gift of your attention, free from expectation.

'Compelling' means having a great 'elevator pitch.' This is no more than two sentences describing what you are offering, whether it is a product, service or your expertise for a job. Job hunters need this; imagine finding yourself in an elevator with the one person who could instantly offer you a job. Would you stand there silently, hoping he would speak to you? Or would you instead have your pitch defined and memorized, so you could engage if given the opportunity?

Finally, you have to close. Unlike sales, you aren't asking someone directly to give you a check. This may make it easier for you. But you do want to make your request and ask for help. Closing should also include the next step. "May I call you next week and check in to see what you have learned?" "I'll touch base by email and see if we could talk further about positions at your company." "I'll call tomorrow so you can give me the contact information for the person you think could help me."

What is a network? Freedictionary.com defines it as "An extended group of people with similar interests or concerns who interact and remain in informal contact for mutual assistance or support." The most critical part of the definition is the word "mutual." You get what you put in, so plan to be active and helpful to those in your network. You may believe you don't have much to offer people older and more experienced, but you may be surprised. While they may not have need for your help, they may have a family member or friend who might value your knowledge.

It's important to understand how a 'favor bank' works. You can't withdraw much beyond what you put in. This doesn't mean you have to help someone else find a job before they will help you. But it does mean that they have to want to help you. Listening with genuine interest to someone else counts as a deposit to your account. Leading with your own needs is a withdrawal, and, as Maclain discovered, he was overdrawn on his favor account.

There are two kinds of networks:

1. Real – in-person networking. This is in some ways easier and in other ways harder. You can make stronger and deeper connections in person. But it takes more time, more effort and, for some, meeting strangers is very hard.
2. Virtual – online networking through social networks, blogs, Twitter and email. These are where the real power lays now, especially with LinkedIn.

Many of us have difficulty when we try to meet new people. We may think that they won't want to know us or—worse—that they may judge us. It probably seemed a lot easier when you were in school where you inevitably found yourself talking to others in class and over time, building friendships. But, even then, you didn't become best friends with everyone you met. Yes, there is a risk to reaching out, but the rewards are potentially great.

When you attend any kind of event, remember that even if the event is not for networking, most people arrive hoping to meet someone interesting. If you bring friends and hang with them, you miss out on the chance to meet someone new. Each encounter is an opportunity, if you choose to look at it that way.

Tara attended an exercise conference in Las Vegas with a few friends, her first time in the city. At first, she hung with her friends from breakfast till bedtime. However, she began to realize that as much fun as she was having, none of this would lead to meeting new people. She needed to land a job, as did her friends. While they hung around together, they never met anyone, except some young men looking for something other than career talk. She knew she had to change something.

The second day, she chose a different class than her friends and made a point of talking with some of the older class members. They all shared a love of the exercise program, which gave her a lead to begin a conversation. They chatted, laughed and worked out together and after class, two asked her if she wanted to go for a coffee. One of them asked Tara where she worked and she confessed that she had just graduated and was looking for a job. She gave her elevator pitch as to what she had to offer and what she wanted to find.

"You know, my company is looking for people with your education. We have a management training program. Is that something you might be interested in?"

Tara felt sure this offer would never have come if she had either stayed with her friends or had started the conversation by telling them she was looking for a job. The three shared a common bond—their love of this exercise class—and that bond made it possible to take the next step.

As you begin to think of who you can connect with, it can be helpful to create a categorized diagram. It can help you think of more names. Start with the people closest to you, your family and dearest friends. Next, consider the friends you rarely see, such as people you studied with but may not contact regularly. Finally, think of anyone whose name you know and whose face you remember. The nice part about building networks on LinkedIn is that the system will prompt you with names and faces of people you may know because they are already connected to connections you have made.

To be successful, it helps to have a few ground rules. These will help you make a better connection. All of these apply both to online and real networks.

1. Be clear on your goal. If you are looking for a job, what skills do you offer? What kind of work would you be willing to do? The more specific you are, the more clearly someone can envision how they can help.
2. Understand that you can only take the first step at a meeting. It is unlikely that you will land a job from a single meeting, but could you learn something about

another company? What kinds of jobs do they offer?
What do they need most that they don't already have?
Asking questions can be a powerful approach, but only
if you aren't simply asking 'Do you have a job for me?'

3. Identify what you have to offer. First, you have their
undivided attention and curiosity. What shared interests do you have, outside of work? A connection is a
beginning.

4. Prepare some questions you could ask anyone that you
might meet, just to get the conversation going. Don't
lead with your need. Since so many will just go with
what they want, it can differentiate you from the pack if
you can avoid doing this. Show genuine interest in the
other person and it will be reciprocated. Online, even if
you are only asking for a connection, consider adding a
personal note to it, indicating that you actually looked
at the person's profile.

5. Manage the time. Even if you have found a soul mate, remember that your goal is to meet at least a few people.
Exchange cards, set up a time to meet again, and then
move on. Don't trap your new friend, nor let them trap
you. Online, spend a few minutes a day making new
connections, or deepening the ones you have.

6. The more you need from the encounter, the more you
should listen for an opportunity to give to the other person. Try not to let your agenda drive everything.

QUICK TIP: Patricia Fripp, internationally recognized
speaker, loves to bring a friend as her personal PR (public rela-
tions) agent. They begin by splitting up; then, when her friend

connects with someone, she will approach and her friend will introduce her. "Sam, I'd love you to meet my friend Patricia Fripp–she's spoken at X, Y and Z, and is an amazing resource for those who want to learn to take their speaking to the next level." Then, Patricia will say, "I'm sure my friend has been too modest to tell you about the last few books she wrote. Everyone is talking about. . . ." PR each other, saying things you might never say about yourself. This is a great way to highlight your abilities and accomplishments without feeling uncomfortable or that you are bragging.

Remember that every encounter has the potential to lead to a valued connection. You never know where the person with the answer to your job challenges might be. It isn't uncommon for people to connect with someone on public transportation, waiting at a doctor's office, at the beach, or at the golf range. Sometimes, the best encounters are these, not necessarily scheduled networking events. Use every opportunity.

Though you might find a person who has the potential to become a lifelong friend, one goal is to make connections for your network. The wider and deeper your network, the easier it is to get help when you need it. Get out there, offer your help and be prepared to enjoy your new connections.

"Call it a clan, call it a network, call it a tribe, call it a family. Whatever you call it, whoever you are, you need one."
Jane Howard, writer, *Families*

Summary

A network is simply a large group of people you know who might be able to help you pursue your career dreams. In this job market, having a large network to draw on is critical in being able to land the job you truly desire. Both online and in person, nearly every day, you have a chance to connect with and get to know people who will be instrumental in helping you find a job. Don't miss any opportunity to grow your network.

CHAPTER 7

Research Companies

> *"Believing that you must do something to perfection is a recipe for stress, and you'll associate the stress with the task and thus condition yourself to avoid it."*
> STEVE PAVLINA, WRITER

Everyone knows that you have to know something about the company you apply to. Many people just don't have a methodology that works for them. Years ago, getting quality data was difficult. Now, the information is out there, but what's the best way to proceed?

Pamela typed into the Google search bar the name of the company she most wanted to work for. The results went on for pages, and immediately she felt overwhelmed at the prospect of wading through it all to find what she needed. She ended up looking only at the company website, but even then, wasn't sure how to navigate it for useful information.

It's not like the CEO is going to interview me, she thought. The mission statements and other marketing information didn't seem helpful to her. *I want to work in accounting; accounting is accounting. What do I really need to know?*

Even as a junior accountant, her skills netted her an interview. Arriving at the imposing headquarters, Pamela felt heartened that she had invested in a well-tailored suit for her first real job. As she approached the front desk, she noticed that even the women were dressed in polo shirts and slacks or casual skirts. None of the men wore a suit or tie. Her confidence sank. The receptionist led her into a conference room that looked more like a play school area than an office space, filled as it was with beanbag chairs, what looked like toys and small tables that resembled the old TV trays of the '60s. Her parents still had a set of them.

The interviewer showed her to a real chair, but plopped himself down on an exercise ball, clearly intending to get in a bit of a workout while they talked. As Pamela looked around, she thought of how great it might be to work in this environment, but her initial discomfort registered with people. She didn't get a second interview.

While it might once have been useful to simply review the annual report of a company and read a few press releases, now, you need to know more. Fortunately, smart use of that Google search function can provide you what you need without taking up too much time, especially with larger companies. In fact, you should be using this at various points in the process. Before applying for jobs, search for information that helps you see if the company offers what you want in a job. You can discover where they have offices and often if they require everyone to go in each day or have most workers working from home. News items help you see what's important, exciting or troubling about the firm. Look both at those they release (generally press releases) and those others write commenting on the company. Also, check out how the website makes you feel–look at their company website as well as their public/consumer site, if they have both. Is there a professional, by-the-books feel to the site? Or is it casual, even fun?

Go to http://finance.yahoo.com and look up the company. Not only is there all the basic financial information, but you can also tap into their message board, which may offer some additional insights, as many of the contributors may be employees. In addition, http://www.glassdoor.com may offer some insights as to the employee experience.

Consider checking out their Twitter feed and Facebook page. The employees assigned to respond to the queries operate under corporate guidelines. How responsive are they to public feedback? Do you like how they respond? How much do they understand and use social media? For many younger job-seekers, these things matter and you can easily check out where they are on this journey. If your aim is to help in social media, a bad showing here would offer an opportunity.

Many companies engage in a great deal of charitable activity and make donations. Since they are likely to be proud of their efforts, you can generally learn about what they support on their website or in news feeds. For some, this involvement may matter a great deal in terms of what it says about their corporate values. If you care, check it out. All companies do something, but you can often distinguish the usual from the things that are close to their heart by looking at their press releases and news items. What activities do employees participate in? The real investment is in human interaction.

Identifying the C-suite person who would be in charge of your department allows you to get some background on that person through LinkedIn and similar sites. LinkedIn will also let you snoop around a little to see who you might know at that company or if one of your primary contacts knows someone. That contact can be a great source of information about corporate politics, culture, values and work-life balance. Best bets are people in similar roles, as different departments may have their own internal culture that differs from the public persona.

If the company publishes articles (many do), check out a few of them in the areas that interest you. Again, while you learn about their sphere of knowledge, you also learn what matters to them.

Zeke's first-choice company set him up for five interviews in one day. A bit intimidated, he decided to arm himself with as much information on the interviewers as he could get. One of the co-worker interviewers was with a man who had a passion for surfing, just as he did. Zeke envied his international travel; the man's Pinterest page showed him surfing in exotic locations all over the world. The manager he hoped to work for still volunteered for a charity group he had worked for while in college. These cues and others gave him conversational openings and powerful connections to the team he wanted to join.

At first, Zeke had no interest in digging through all the data, but as he searched, the people he knew he had to speak with became real to him. Seeing faces, looking at references, looking at hobbies, he began to feel he already knew some of them, at least enough to feel a lot more comfortable when they first met.

Once you land an interview, check out the people you will speak with. This is where you can learn some great information about their background and common ground you may have with them. The prior research also helps to show you the way they talk about things—the language they use. Review it before an interview so you can sound like one of the gang. Subtle gestures can go a long way to helping them see you as already part of the team. The information you have gathered also helps you pose smart and useful questions that will help you understand if this is a good fit for you. Interviewers will notice that you did your homework; use it, but don't flaunt it.

Before accepting an offer, review your file of information on the company. How do you feel about their products and services? Their mission? Although you might have deplored pizza, even as you made it to pay your way through college, your career is better served by working for a company you are proud to represent. Every employee is another 'face of the company' and, as such, when people know you work there, they will assess or reassess their view of the company based on what they see in you. You need to share their passions, their energy and their goals in order to shine. Make sure you know that this isn't just 'a' job, but the right job for you, at this point in time.

Why research? Aside from the significant advantage it gives you going into your interview, it also ensures that you know enough to decide if the job is a good fit. While early on in a career it is expected that you might try out various jobs, switching jobs often because you have made too many wrong choices can make people question your commitment and abilities. Take a little more time, do a little more homework and ensure that each position you take will provide a springboard for your career, an opportunity to grow and introduce you to people you want to spend time around.

Summary

Researching companies is so much easier now that you have no excuse not to know everything you can about the companies you apply to. By investing the time, you demonstrate to employers that you care about their company, which is an essential element in landing the job. They want you to want to work for them, not just the first company that offers you a job. Show your interest; take the time to learn.

CHAPTER 8

Creating a Personal Brand

> "A brand is a living entity-and it is enriched or undermined cumulatively over time, the product of a thousand small gestures."
> MICHAEL EISNER, CEO

Branding is a hot topic everywhere, but what is it exactly? Your personal brand is the words people choose to describe you. For many years, only products and services had brands. Without much thought, we know the difference in the branding behind Rock Star and Pepsi. As the image of clone-like businessmen of the '50s fades from memory, the cult of personality is everywhere now, fostered by reality TV. What this means is that employers are no longer so much looking for cookie-cutter robots, but are interested and concerned about who you really are.

Whether you have thought about your brand before or to-day is the first time you thought about branding, you already have one or more brands. Your family might describe you one way, your friends another. When you don't consider that this establishes your 'brand,' you cede control to them. It's much better to consciously create the brand you want for a given situation. This doesn't mean not being you, but being the 'you' that best supports your goals. Think of yourself as a multi-faceted, many-sided diamond. While all views might be wonderful, each angle is different. You can choose to display the set of facets that works best in any given situation. You're still you.

The elements that go into a brand begin with your appearance, including how you dress, your cleanliness habits, your hair style, and how you carry yourself. How you speak and how you use body language also contribute to the way people view you. It can be useful to ask for constructive comments on how your friends and family see you and what words they would use to describe you. Is that the image you wish to project? None of us see ourselves as clearly as others do—get the input and adjust as necessary.

Josea had made good money as a musician during college and, to support the image, had crafted a 'musician' brand that worked for him. Once out of school, he found himself too comfortable with his well-maintained 'dreads' and casual clothes. He considered himself laid-back, friendly and casual—all components of himself he really liked. Then one day a friend called him a slacker. Startled, he asked what he meant.

"Well, you look like you never have to work hard. You just laze around, pick up your axe when you feel like it or need some bread. I didn't mean to diss you."

Josea mulled over the word 'slacker.' If employers thought that, who would hire him? While he liked some elements of that description, it also negated the hard work he put into crafting songs, honing his ability to coax beautiful music from his guitar, and the time he spent lining up gigs. He wasn't lazy. But if even a friend thought he was, he knew he had to change his image.

Who did he want to be? As he began to look for work, he developed a brand that took the best of who he had been in college combined with the more mature, business-focused musician he had become. Still unwilling to consider real business attire, he found a way to make his somewhat grubby style look like a fashion statement by simply buying nicer items and ensuring they were clean and ironed. People began to describe him as creative and a thinker. Relieved, Josea realized he didn't have to be someone else, just the best 'him' he could be.

Many companies have expanded the realm of acceptable dress to include casual slacks and skirts, leaving the suits and ties behind. While it won't be a disaster to be a little more formal than the company's style—and, in fact, it is a good idea to go a little dressier—you want to demonstrate with your image that you already fit in. In the creative arts and start-ups, casual is more acceptable, but you'd never want to wear jeans to an interview, even your nicest ones.

While this seems like a trivial detail, the reality is that people make up their minds about how they see you within the first 30 seconds. This sets the bar. Your behavior, your voice and your body language all adjust their perception in the next few minutes. You only get to show your competence, experience and expertise further down the conversational road. At this point, they may have already decided you're not the right person. Practicing your 'first impression' in front of friends will make it second nature when you interview and ensure that these concerns don't add to the inevitable nervousness.

How do you create the best brand for yourself? There are many possibilities and methods for formulating your brand, but they all start with how you need to be seen to be successful in your career. If you network with people in your prospective field, observe them and emulate them. Understand the type of people they work with and hope to attract to join them. Understanding this might also help you figure out where you might best fit in. At some sites, you're encouraged to dress as your favorite 'Big Bang Theory' character. Others prefer you look and act a little more formal.

A personal brand is simply the way you are seen by colleagues, peers and managers, but you have the opportunity to define it when you understand how it is created. Your brand is a synthesis of the following four elements, only some of which you can demonstrate during interviews:

1. How you show up [timeliness, dress, personal hygiene, attitude, body language, vocal tone, etc.]
2. How you do your job [thoroughly, on-time, within budget]

3. What skills you offer [technical, management, organizational]
4. What makes you special or unique [differentiation]

Your brand is your public persona—it is not your personality. Your default behavior tends to rely on habits and patterns you have developed over the years. If it isn't serving you, it is time to look at what behaviors may be holding you back. Behaviors that served you when you were younger or in a different role may no longer serve you in achieving your goals. You can choose how you want to be viewed and your 'brand' can be different for different situations or professions. As an example, banking probably requires a little more formality than writing code for Facebook.

Ashwanda had tons of student debt, so she didn't have the money to buy a lot of interview clothes. Still, she knew that the clothes that had been sufficient for attending class and going to casual parties wouldn't hit the mark. She wanted flexibility, so she went to a consignment store and looked for some basic clothes she could mix and match. A tweed jacket and two skirts with two matching blouses didn't cost much, and the fabric was good quality. It showed her taste. To reflect her personality, she found a discount store and included some casual jewelry that not only helped people see who she was as a person, but also allowed her to make her few outfits look like more. Some consignment shops also had shoes to enhance her new image.

Still, she felt like this wasn't enough. She got together with a few college friends and they took turns walking, sitting, and being observed while they carried on a conversation.

Each discovered habits they wanted to work on before they went for their first interview. Ashwanda learned how to sit with a skirt on; it took time to feel comfortable crossing just her ankles. LeShel realized she messed with her hair when she felt nervous. Michaela suggested she pull it back so she wasn't so tempted. By assessing each other as if they were meeting a stranger for the first time, they had the chance to create the image they wanted to project, not the one they defaulted to.

Is your brand what you want it to be? It's important to know where you are first, then to decide what you want your brand to be.

Exercise 8-1: Ask friends and family what they would say if they had to describe you to a stranger who needed a lot of detail to find you. Would it be different if they were hoping to introduce you to with a friend? Note the points you don't like hearing. In a few days, look objectively at the descriptions and consider what kinds of job roles you could see this person fitting into. Is this who you want to be? Are these the roles you want to play?

What are you looking for as you work on your personal brand? Though we've focused so far on more superficial aspects, brand includes more than that. Demonstrating intelligence and knowledge can be most easily accomplished by silence and great listening skills, punctuated by the occasional injection of brilliance. Asking well-thought-out questions can also contribute to that image. When trying to figure out how you want to be perceived, consider what you would want to hear if you happened to eavesdrop on a conversation about you. Does this match how you show up now?

What do you offer an employer? What we offer is no longer limited to highlights noted on our résumés. Companies are beginning to truly value what was previously dismissed as the soft or right-brain (creative) skills. Are you the accounting guru? Do you manage projects superbly? Or are you valued for your agility in learning and getting up to speed fast? Your ability to work as part of a team, to respond quickly and robustly to change and to align with corporate goals may be more important to your longevity than your left-brain (logical) skills.

You also need to look at the difference between what you value in yourself and what people recognize you for. Is there something you would love people to know about you? Are there gaps between what you can offer and what you would like to be able to offer? Communication skills, both written and verbal, are very important. In our IM and email world, people are not always aware of the image they present in these short messages. It is all a part of how you are viewed, so text accordingly. Casual conversations are another trap. Do you forget yourself when you begin to get comfortable with someone?

An important element is your distinctive competence. What makes you special? We all have special gifts, but too often, in an attempt to fit into the corporate world, we dismiss or downplay them. Or we don't realize the importance of identifying and celebrating these skills. You might be the best at explaining complex technical concepts to business people, or one of the few who can talk mainframe, UNIX and Windows, for example. Perhaps you are gifted at arbitration: the one person who can achieve a win-win when people are at odds with each other. Your distinctive competence is at the core of your brand; when you discover what sets you apart, you can market this to ensure your place *wherever* you want to be. The biggest challenge is really being clear on your gifts and understanding how you can use them to benefit your organization. Once you identify your distinctive competence, it will be easy to show your value to others.

A clear, positive brand identifies you as someone companies want on their team. Defining and honing your brand is a task worth doing. When you establish your brand, you control your destiny.

Summary

Whether you know it or not, you have a brand. Understand how people view you and then tailor your image to match the way you wish to be viewed. Control the message. Ensure that the wonderful person you are inside is reflected in every external aspect.

CHAPTER 9

Managing Your Brand
with Technology

> "Silence speaks so much louder than
> screaming tantrums. Never give anyone
> an excuse to say that you're crazy."
> — TAYLOR SWIFT, SINGER

Unless you are in the business of managing publicity, most of us don't really know what to do next with the brand we've created. How do we ensure that we keep the good image we have developed? Before the Internet, keeping control of your personal information and managing your brand was relatively easy. Now, with smart phone cameras everywhere, you may find questionable pictures of yourself online. 'Friends' may talk about you in ways you don't like. The problem comes when employers search your name and find these images and comments. And they will. What will they see?

Janice had done all her homework. Her education and volunteer work made her a great candidate for an event planner position. She found and applied to a number of entry-level jobs. Happy to have found openings, she counted herself luckier than her friends.

But, even when she achieved an interview, it didn't result in an offer. What had she done wrong? An older friend, hearing her story, took a look at her social presence. "Janice," she said. "Look here. You've been tagged by so many people at parties, looking. . .well, less than professional. At the same time, you're not where you need to be. You aren't even on LinkedIn."

Janice reviewed the pictures, got the tags removed and, more important, changed her privacy settings to make it harder for someone to happen across the pictures. It had never occurred to her that someone other than her Facebook friends and family would ever look at these images.

Some prospective employers are asking job candidates to provide LinkedIn and Facebook IDs and passwords. Privacy cases are moving through the court, but you could run into this. Even if they don't ask, there is a lot of information visible to the public in Facebook profiles. Privacy settings are changed frequently by Facebook and other social sites, so you need to check them out on a regular basis.

The safest bet is to assume that, whatever you post, it is permanent and visible. As valuable a tool as the Internet is for increasing your network of friends, it's also dangerous turf, littered with landmines for those who do not understand what is visible and to whom. Too many people think they can maintain a separate professional and personal image. That is a dangerous conceit online. Even back in the '90s when the Internet was not a big factor in the work-place, some people lost their jobs over their postings or the sites they had searched on their work PC. Public is public.

So what can you do to protect your brand? The same tools that can expose you are also the places to further define and strengthen your brand. Here are the key areas to consider.

1. **Set up Google Alerts:** Set up a regular schedule of Google Alerts to track the use of your name. Don't forget to set up alerts for any of the various ways your name might be spelled or referenced on the Net, including setting one with your middle initial. Get a weekly report and make sure your name (and all its versions) doesn't appear in a context that makes you uncomfortable. If you find a problem, you can request the site to cease and desist by contacting them directly. If the mention is untrue, you should be able to convince them to remove the information. You can't eliminate all mentions, but at least you know what's out there. If you can see it, so can others. You can set up alerts easily. Go to www.google.com/alerts.

2. **Join LinkedIn:** LinkedIn is the number one site to be on if you're in the market for a job. You should be a member of LinkedIn, and any other career site related to your prospective field. These sites are your online professional presence and employers expect to find you here. It's a great place to attract interest with a well-crafted profile, which acts as a résumé. LinkedIn requires an invitation from someone to join, but given that it has been around a while, it shouldn't be hard to find someone to ask you.

LinkedIn is free, but someone has to pay for it. In this case, it's recruiters, HR departments and the like. So you know they are looking at it to find candidates for jobs.

You may have joined LinkedIn while at college and joined your college network. That's a great start. Now, look for other interest groups relating to your career ambitions. If you didn't connect while in college, do it now. Many of these groups are great for referrals.

Once you join, begin getting "LinkedIn" with friends and colleagues. A good, strong presence can help you in your career. If you don't have a profile here or it doesn't reflect the same things as your résumé, you can have some problems.

LinkedIn also allows you to have ready access to favorable references. To get references, offer to recommend your colleagues. Current and former co-workers, fellow students and managers may be happy to exchange references to beef up their own reputation.

Join professional groups on LinkedIn to connect with people in your desired profession. These groups share all kinds of information and can help you learn more about companies, openings and the work in that field.

QUICK TIP: For those new to LinkedIn, there are many useful webcasts and how-to guides on the LinkedIn site as well as elsewhere on the Internet. Play a few of these to learn how you can get the most out of your networking experience.

3. **Manage Facebook:** Building your network? Reconnect with old friends and deepen connections with current ones. But be cautious. A large friend list isn't necessarily a good thing. Make sure that those who can see you online are part of your 'trust' network. Check your privacy settings often. Facebook is notorious for changing the

rules, and what was once private may not be anymore. Be extremely cautious about using applications or accepting surveys, as many of these constitute "opting in" for the purposes of sharing your information. Put no content out there that you wouldn't want a stranger to see. This includes pictures, as well as your profile and updates.

4. **Use Twitter:** Twitter is even more public than Facebook; anyone can read what you post even if they do not follow you, so you will get more visibility. Even if you do little with your site, once you set up a presence, you will find yourself being "followed." If you **want** to be followed, be interesting and share useful tips and information. If you enjoy a lively discussion, make sure the information you share fits your brand. You have a wonderful opportunity to showcase your versatility, intelligence and expertise, but you also have a great chance to make mistakes here. If you want a Twitter account that lets "you be you," make sure that it isn't tied to the business-branded image you already have. Use a second account with a catchy user ID that isn't your name. You can have several Twitter IDs for different purposes.

5. **Watch Out for Picture Phones** – Today, most phones provide both video and still camera capabilities. As soon as a picture is snapped, it can be online in minutes. Some new phones come equipped with a "Facebook" button to automatically upload your latest shot. Be aware of individuals taking pictures, especially if you're in a crowd situation, such as a party. Try to behave as if your mother is watching you–since almost everyone is on the Net,

she very well may be. Don't assume your friends won't take your picture. What seems funny to someone now might haunt you later. Too many find themselves the next YouTube sensation. They're so easy to post, but often very hard to delete. Consider suggesting a photo-free zone at parties so those who want privacy can have it. It isn't possible to completely control your image, but you need to try.

What else can hurt your brand?

Fernando had been blogging and Tweeting for years. He felt sure he presented a good image while enjoying the chance to be controversial on some of his alternate user-ids. What he hadn't considered is how many people knew these 'alter egos' were him. It wasn't hard for employers to trace back and find posts that made him less desirable as a candidate.

Exercise 9-1: Pick a friend or colleague who appears to have a lively social life. Google them. Check out their public presence on Facebook. If you are a friend and logon as yourself, you will see everything they share. Look at LinkedIn. Did you learn something surprising about your friend? Note the positive information you found, and also note the kinds of things that might change how you felt about that person. This might help you see better what you want to avoid for your own online presence.

Brand management means watching for the small errors that chip away at your professional image. Here are some areas to watch for.

1. **Email Etiquette:** Be cautious with the "Reply All" button unless you need to send the response to everyone on the list. Watch your spelling and grammar. Many employers and headhunters said they would pass on a candidate who had a single error in his or her résumé. Emails are even more problematic as they're so easy to write quickly. Use spell-check, but use your eyes, too. Reread every email before sending it. Though the bar is lower for emails, frequent mistakes make people doubt you. Treat emails like any hard-copy communication. Skip texting abbreviations; make sure every sentence is readable to your audience. Use your best writing here. Clean, concise emails will make you stand out. Great communication skills are highly valued in the business world, and emails are part of that package. (Learn more about email in Chapter 22.

QUICK TIP: Address your email *last*. If you inadvertently hit "send," it will go nowhere. It gives you more time to think and review your word choice.

2. **Text and IM Etiquette:** Use these vehicles for a quick question or to set up a time for a call. Although texting and instant messaging are valuable business tools, they're too often abused. Are you using them productively or simply annoying a co-worker? As you would with a phone call, ask if it's a good time for a conversation. People don't always remember to change their status, and no one can function with constant interruptions. When texting or IMing, don't expect an

immediate response. People often leave their IM status open and their cell phones on even when they aren't available. Respect that. Try to remember to start by asking them if they have a moment for you. If you absolutely, positively must reach someone, call them at the number they prefer.

QUICK TIP: Make a note of people's preferences for engagement. Some people prefer a phone call. Others are fine with an IM introduction for quick answers, but prefer email for less time-critical issues. You shouldn't try to change them. Respect these differences. Interact with others at work according to their preferences.

3. **Technological Multi-tasking:** The greatest compliment you can give to a person is your full attention, which is impossible if you're dividing it. When you're talking with someone, listen to them. If you text or take a call during a conversation, you're basically saying that other things are more important than they are. Turn off your electronic annoyances, or at least mute them. If you're expecting a call, let the other person know at the beginning of the conversation and then end the call quickly.

What you're telling them when you put technology first is that you're a person who doesn't respect others. Today, the way you use technology depicts who you are. Remember that anything on the Internet, no matter how transitory it may appear, is probably more permanent than the crazy hairdo from your college years. Once, you only had to worry about what your neighbors thought. Now, your neighbor is the world.

"Your brand is what people say about you when you're not in the room."
Jeff Bezos, CEO

Summary
Your social presence is the first place employers look. LinkedIn is a powerful way to look good to an employer, but Facebook, Instagram, Pinterest, and Twitter are places where your image may not be what you want.

A final note on technology: once you're employed, you will likely be provided with a PC and perhaps a cell phone. It's important to note that, while everyone uses these devices for some small amount of personal activity, your employer does have the right to look at what's on them. In some cases, a lot of things you can do on your own devices are blocked at work, but some may not be. When you try to access sites and capabilities that are blocked, a record is kept of the attempt. Make sure that you keep your personal interactions on your own devices as much as possible. People have been terminated by misuse of corporate technology.

How you interact, through email, telephone and texting will create a lasting image to those receiving your communications. Make sure it's the one you want. Treat all communications with the same respect you would have face-to-face.

Landing
Your Job

CHAPTER 10

What Doesn't Work

> "My heroes are the ones who survived
> doing it wrong, who made mistakes,
> but recovered from them."
> — BONO, SINGER

When you start on a new venture, it can help to know upfront some of the things that don't work well. Not every lesson has to be learned by you personally; that's just too painful. While each of the ideas mentioned here have worked in a small number of cases, they aren't the most productive way to go about getting a job.

The first is the unsolicited job application. Before the Internet, most people would find a job listing in the newspaper or hear about a job and then apply for it in person. Now, most companies have open job requisitions available to all online with the ability to apply just a key-stroke away. It can be tempting. Why leave home when you can sit at your PC or tablet and apply for 100 jobs in just a few hours? It seems to make sense, and also seems to match what companies want you to do.

While this might be a somewhat viable approach in a market where the number of candidates is small relative to the openings, it simply doesn't work in the market we're in.

> Every day, Brandon put his full attention for several hours on completing job applications. His mother told all her friends how diligent he was. "Brandon is going to get a terrific job. He's open to moving, looking at all the major companies, and has the credentials to back it up," she said.
>
> As true as her statements were about Brandon, they didn't reflect reality in the market. Brandon never got a single email or call to set up an interview. After weeks of work, he had nothing to show for it but bleary eyes and the sense that he had been misled about his viability in the market. And yet, Brandon had real skills and a few internships to demonstrate his experience. But no one seemed to notice.

Looking at the current hiring process from the perspective of an employer helps to demonstrate the problem. For any given job, thousands may apply. Newspapers cover the in-person hiring fairs and show pictures of the long lines. Online, it can be hard to envision your competition, but it's there. No company has the resources or people to screen all those applications. Just as you use a computer to fill out the application, they are using one to screen you out. Yes, to screen you out.

In order to winnow the list to the most likely candidates, online job applications are designed to find ways to eliminate as many applicants as possible. What may appear to be an innocuous question may instead be a land mind. While there are rules governing interviews, some companies even include questions they aren't legally allowed to ask, such as age, race, sex, etc. But in the course of working through 10-12 pages of questions, it can be easy to simply answer them all rather than to see the application for what it is.

When you complete hundreds of online job applications, you may have simply wasted your time. Unless you have an unusual skill and the experience to back it up, this process is a sieve with very large holes designed to ensure you fall through. Though ample proof in the market exists, I tested it by applying to two jobs tailor-made to my abilities and experience. I submitted these applications late on a Friday afternoon, but on Sunday morning got emails indicating that I didn't have the skills or experience required. Want to know which land mine I stepped on? In my case, it was age. You had to include your birthdate.

When should you fill out an online job application? Only do this when an employer asks you to do so, and only after he has had a chance to speak with you and review your skills. At this point, your job application becomes part of the record and is needed prior to hiring. The personal connection can ensure that your application bypasses the 'sieve' and goes directly to a person who can fairly assess you.

The second mistake is assuming that the posted jobs are the only jobs available. Most HR consultants and experts in the field estimate that the hidden job market comprises 80% while the visible market is only 20%. If you only look at the posted jobs, you've missed a ton of opportunities. In part because of the huge numbers of applicants relative to positions available, many companies don't post jobs until they have an idea of who they want. In some cases, the jobs are first open to existing employees, yet with a good network you may learn of them ahead of the field. Other jobs have long dropped off the active hiring list because the company never found a good candidate. Still others represent work that needs to be done but hasn't yet been defined as a job. The 80% not only represents a lot more jobs than appear to be available; it also represents a market few are actually tapping.

The more powerful your network, the more likely you will be to find out about these jobs or even have a job created for you. While the latter sounds almost impossible, it happens every day. A great candidate not only knows what they have to offer a company but also what the company needs, including capabilities they never considered. Every day, successful applicants have built a case that there is a hole, a missing piece, that when filled by them will help the company achieve even more success.

Asad didn't have a large LinkedIn network, but what he lacked in numbers he had covered in terms of cornering his niche market. Through MeetUp groups, training, and other social connections while he attended college, he had built a network of people who were experts in his field. In his senior year, he began reaching out to his network, asking where he might find a job. He had taken the time to be clear on how his skills could be utilized in his industry, so he wasn't asking for just any job. He knew what he had to offer.

Asad's network recognized this as well, and a few connections came through with introductions to managers at their companies. He knew what jobs were publicly advertised at these companies, but instead of being limited to a few openings, he found himself offered interviews to do jobs that he had never seen listed. While his friends struggled to find anyone to speak with, Asad struggled only to find the time to talk to his many contacts and follow up on all the opportunities. He had the luxury of waiting until the right spot came along and, with his connections, had the ability to land that job.

The third mistake is not taking charge of your job search. In a good market, it's possible to rely on headhunters to find you great jobs. It's possible, but it isn't always the best way. After all, they will only present you with jobs where they will get paid for matching a candidate to a position. In the current market, you should talk to headhunters, if they exist in your profession, but you must do more. Too many don't realize how challenging this will be. Armed with a diploma from a fine institution and the praise of family and friends, you might begin to believe that companies just can't wait to hire you. While this might be true once they learn about you, it's up to you to ensure that you get past the electronic gatekeepers and in to the person who can make that decision.

Part of the way you may default your responsibility to take charge is by simply asking people to tell you about possible jobs. This technique may have been how you got the waitressing job or the pizza-making job, but it won't be as helpful here. You need to be very specific about the kind of job you want and make some effort to see if your connection's company even offers this kind of job. You have to do your homework first. You need to understand why people won't or can't help you.

Most people don't have the time to scan their job sites for possibilities. They may care deeply about you, but they don't know what you want.   You're the expert on this. A simple request, such as: "Can you find something that might be good for me at your company?", isn't simple to the person hearing it. In reality, how would they know even if they looked at the career site? This is particularly true if you are asking about a job in an area they know little about. HR job descriptions don't always help. And it takes a lot of time to go through all the listings at a large company.

You have to be clear and have a job or jobs in mind. Don't think of asking for help until you've reviewed the site and noted specifics of the jobs you think might be a good fit. At this point, you can ask your contacts for help in applying to these specific jobs. In many companies, referrals pay off for the person referring you, so there is an incentive to help you. But you have to help yourself first.

For those jobs that aren't listed, you first need to spot a need and then make it clear how you could fill it. When you build the case, your friends can help you get in to talk to someone who could see your value.

A final mistake would be insisting that the only option is a full-time, salaried job. Internships, temporary jobs and contract-to-hire are increasingly offered as possibilities and may be a fast way to career success for you. Given the difficulty in firing people, many companies now prefer to minimize their initial investment in new hires. By working at an 'apprenticeship,' you can earn your way to a position you couldn't have otherwise accessed. Offer a trial. It might be the thing that separates you from everyone else.

Take ownership of your job search. Control it, manage it and expect to do most of the work. No one cares more than you do about finding you a job. But when you care enough to do the work upfront, you'll find people who will help you take a step forward on the search.

"We are not born to wait. We are born to do."
– Dean Koontz, writer, Your Heart Belongs to Me

Summary
There are a few things that can cause you problems in your job search. Resolve now to:

- Only fill out online job applications when asked to do so by an employer or in the rare case where the job pool is likely to be small because you have unique skills
- Not limit your job hunting to jobs posted on employer or job sites. There are many more jobs out there than what are posted. Use your network to find them.
- Look for openings you can fill. Jobs may be created for you when you can identify a need and show how you can make a difference to a company
- Own your job search. Be clear on exactly what you are looking for whenever you ask someone for help. The better you do with this, the more people can help you and the more they are likely to want to do so
- Open your mind up to possibilities other than a regular, salaried position. This might be your eventual goal, but in today's market, other options may directly lead you to that, if you're open to considering them.

CHAPTER 11

Exploiting Your Network

> "I think fearless is having fears
> but jumping anyway."
> TAYLOR SWIFT, SINGER

Once you have a virtual and physical network, you now need to understand how to use it. As important as building the network is, how you use it may be even more critical. Using your network is a withdrawal from the 'Favor Bank,' so you have to make sure you don't get too badly overdrawn. Invest in relationships so that when you need them, you can rely on them. It's also important to learn how to ask.

David had always been lucky with summer jobs. His father had a wealth of contacts and they were ready to offer him a position—hard work and often less-than-optimal pay—but he found that he learned more and earned more than his friends.

And it didn't hurt that he never got stuck working fast food or clerking in a store.

Once he graduated with a degree in computer science, he again hoped to have help from his father's friends, many of whom had contacts at the places he most wanted to work. He wrote up a résumé, but even to his eyes, it appeared a jumble of the odd jobs and volunteer work he had done. At the next gathering of family friends, he began asking his contacts to help him find a job. "Do you know of anything that would work for me?" he said, not wanting to appear too picky.

Although each man took his résumé, he never heard back from any of them. Saddened, he began to apply for jobs online, again frustrated when no interviews resulted. David wondered if perhaps he had done something wrong, but he had no idea what it could be. The same men who had gotten him jobs in the past suddenly seemed to have no interest in helping him now.

Marshall Goldsmith, a premiere executive coach, has a book entitled, "What Got You Here Won't Get You There." The strategies we used to get summer jobs aren't the same as the ones we need for career jobs. When looking for occasional or part-time work, people are less concerned with what you want to do, what your abilities are or what you plan to do in the future. The only question to be asked is: "Can you do the job now?" In that sense, although there is a lot of competition for those jobs and no real way to stand out, getting low-end jobs is actually easier than getting a career job.

David's request failed for a variety of reasons. First, he really had no idea what kind of job he hoped to land. It's essential not only to figure out what kinds of work you can do with the training and education you have, but also to do the homework to figure out what that job is called at a variety of companies. Otherwise, you're asking the person to not only help you land a job, but also to figure out what job you should get. As an adult beginning your career, people expect you to have a vision for what this looks like and to have done some research first. You may have several possibilities that will work, but you need to know and communicate this. This particular problem plagues people of all ages in all lines of work. Laid off, they call everyone they know and ask, "Can you help me find a job?" Even the most caring person is going to be stymied. What kind of job would he want? Where does he want to work? You can't ask that of them. You need to know.

For business, you have two great online networks. LinkedIn is the most powerful tool for job seekers and provides a wealth of ways to find people at companies where you want to work. You can ask for introductions to people who are LinkedIn to people in your primary network. But Facebook has recently added a feature that could also be of help. Search for "my friends who work for x company", indicating the company you have an interest in. Many people have different LinkedIn and Facebook networks, so be sure to try both. Another way to use Facebook is to search for people who work in an industry or have a specific interest or a specific title. Again, it's all about building a strong network to help you get a foot in the door where you want or, at the least, to provide you with information you'll need to land a job.

Before you approach your network, figure out what kind of job you want. Demonstrate your initiative by doing the work and figuring out as much as possible about where you belong.

Ideally, you should look for specific jobs at companies that interest you. When you have that, it's much easier for someone to help you with an introduction, a rave review to be put on your profile, etc. Since many jobs aren't posted, you don't necessarily need that, but if you can phrase the type of job in the Human Resources vernacular, it makes it much easier for someone to help you.

You must also know how you expect them to help. Are you asking them to submit your application as an employee to a specific job? Make an introduction to the hiring manager? Give you some insight into how the company functions? There are many ways someone can help, but only you can tell them what it is that you need from them. Don't make them guess.

The 'Favor Bank' works somewhat like a bank but unlike a bank, people aren't usually maintaining a careful balance. Still, it makes a difference that you are remembered for being a friend, being helpful, and for offering aid.

Tangible deposits include performing a courtesy on social sites. First, for those you know well in the workplace, write a review for them on LinkedIn. Reviews are very valuable to people's careers. Many people only write reviews for peers or for employees, but employees like to see that a manager is so well liked that people will go the extra mile for them. Make sure to select areas in which they excel–it's so easy to just click on a few of them, adding to the value of their LinkedIn profile. Connect with people you want to work with and share your network. Pass on useful links and videos judiciously. Let your social presence be one of a 'giver,' not a promoter. Look for ways to give, and you will be positively remembered.

The same is true of your real-world network. Are you the one always asking someone to drive you somewhere, pick up items for you, tell you about the homework assignment you missed? Or are you the go-to person who not only does these things, but looks for opportunities to help? There are countless stories of someone who helped someone without any thought of what it might do for them. Later, they learn that their act brought them to the attention of someone who could really make a difference to their career.

Leah got excited about fundraising sites such as KickStarter after she saw a friend get her credit card bills paid off by strangers. Still, to her that somehow seemed wrong. However, after a summer spent helping build a school building in Mexico, she had wondered how they would get the books to fill their library. She also knew that a lot of the students had to share textbooks. Money would help each student have one of their own. She found a number of sites designed for non-profit fund-raising and created a video montage of the pictures she had taken onsite. She wrote up her plan and posted it. In only a few days, she had raised enough to fill the library twice over.

Delighted to be able to add to the project she had started, she began wondering what she could do next. The local paper reported her ventures and, to her surprise, she began getting inquiries as to what she wanted to do for a career. Representatives of local companies commented on her ability to write great website content. They loved her short video. Leah hadn't exactly worked out where she wanted to start, but quickly began to put together a career idea based on what she felt best about in her volunteer projects. It didn't take her long to land a job.

The magic of the Favor Bank is that you don't necessarily have to do a favor for someone for that person to recognize you and reward you. Leah hadn't done her project to land a job; she really wanted to finish a project she had started. But in giving to others, she shone a light on her skills. In this case, she didn't even need to build a network: her social presence was her network.

Some other rules of networking are that all interactions from you should be one-on-one. This means no mass emails asking for help. As tempting as it is, and as easy as the technology makes it, sending spam to people isn't going to yield results. Whether in person, on the phone or on line, every interaction should begin with a clear statement of who you are and why you are calling, followed by your specific request. You have to prepare. Know what that person can do that no one else could do for you. Demonstrate that you have done your homework. You know what you want to work at, you know what it's called, and your résumé reflects that objective.

When it's someone you don't know well, make your 'ask' small at first. Although most people love to help others, when they don't know you, they're not invested in you. Find a way to connect with them, develop a relationship with them, and then ask.

Don't limit yourself to people of your own age. And remember, everyone knows family and friends who work. Your best friend might just have an uncle at Google. Would she be willing to help you? Why not?

The rule of career success is that it isn't what you know but who you know. And the most valuable members of your network are the ones with whom you have developed a real relationship.

"The currency of real networking is not greed but generosity."
Keith Ferrazz, speakeri

Summary

There's a right way and a wrong way to use your network. Remember that when you can offer help to someone else in even a small way, they're more likely to want to help you. And when you make your 'ask,' be sure you have a clear, well-defined request. Don't expect them to do all the work for you. Make it easy for people to help you and you'll be surprised at the response you get.

CHAPTER 12

Informational Interviews

"Enjoy the journey and not just the endgame."
BENEDICT CUMBERBATCH, ACTOR

Many people think of an interview as the talk with a hiring manager that results in a job offer. However, it isn't the only kind of interview that is valuable in your career. The informational interview is a chance to talk with people who might be in a position to hire you, but who may not currently have a position available. The goal of the interview is not necessarily a job; it is to learn about the company, the types of positions available, the needs of the company, and its plans for the future. Sounds just like an interview? It is, but without the expectation that the conversation will lead to a job. In many cases, it is much easier to arrange an informational interview than to land a job interview. However, many informational interviews can lead to jobs. As has been discussed, not every job that is available is actually posted on a job website. Many never make it that far, and it's those jobs, as well as the information you can gather, that make striving for these interviews invaluable.

> Steve had trained in electrical engineering and really wanted to work for a utility company. After several months, he became discouraged because none of the utilities were hiring. He began to consider regions of the country he didn't really want to live in, but the job listings were sparse. He felt frustrated. All that training, all those years in college when he put in the hours in study rather than enjoying the collegiate social life, and he felt like he had wasted his time.
>
> His father knew a man who had a management position at their local utility. They were both members of the local Elks club. His father said, "I can put in a call for you, but this man is way above the level of hiring engineers. It could be worth your time to talk with him, though."
>
> Feeling like there was nothing to lose, he asked his father to make an appointment. When he met the man, Steve launched into his interview mode, leading with his skills and desires for a job. Silences became uncomfortable as he realized the man really didn't care what he was saying. He hadn't prepared any questions, so the meeting was short. Steve didn't know what had gone wrong. "What was I supposed to do?"

Planned and executed well, informational interviews often lead to real interviews, but to do this, you need to understand the crucial differences. Your goal, initially, is information gathering. You want to learn what the company is looking for in terms of skills and experience, understand more about what a day-in-the-life on the job is like, and understand what qualities are critical when they look to hire someone. Though it is natural to speak about yourself a little, the goal is not to show your desire for a job. Remember: you're not talking about a posted job. This is a case where you hope to get the person you are speaking with to do most of the talking so you can learn as much as possible. You should bring paper and a pen and make notes of what you learn. If the interviewer believes that you are pushing him or her to turn this into a job interview, they will cut the interview short.

When you have gathered a lot of information about the company, you can inquire about opportunities. It is at this point that you mention that you are looking for a position doing X, and that you wondered if he/she might know of anything that would be a good match for you. You will have your résumé, available, but not bring it out until he indicates an interest in seeing it. Tie your conversation to the information you have gathered. "I understand that your company is growing rapidly," you might say. "In many cases, this means that you will have to add staff. Is that likely? Would your needs include someone of my ability or someone who could be quickly trained to produce?"

You can also ask if there are other people at the company you can speak with. This is important. Often, the informational interview begins with someone at a senior level of the company, someone who is not likely to be involved in hiring someone beginning their career. But if they sense your interest in the company and feel that you could be a match based on your skills, blend with the corporate culture and interest level, they are more likely to refer you to someone who might have a related position in the future. The big 'ask' here is not for a job, it is for a referral to someone else in the company you can talk to. You may have a variety of these interviews, but if a job might be available in the future, you will eventually talk to the people in charge of the right area. Always be sure to have copies of your résumé and a cover letter.

In some cases, there are no jobs expected in the foreseeable future, but then you have that information as well as a wealth of information about your desired industry. Though we may be clear on what kind of work we want to do, we often don't know much about the company itself and all the things that need doing. You're looking to understand as much as you can about this specific company, its values, its goals, and how it sees its place in the world. You want to learn about how they hire people, who they hire and how they train them.

Be prepared with a list of questions for each interview. As with regular interviews, you can do a lot of research about people online so that you know something about the person you will be speaking with. Prepare almost as fully as you would for a job interview, but focus the attention on what you can learn. Your interest and passion will resonate with the people you talk to. People who love their work enjoy sharing what they know with others; many live to see people light up as they talk about it. Be that person.

Kaneesha's father's best friend worked for the top accounting firm in the city. He agreed to speak with her, but her father warned her, "His time is valuable. He won't have a lot of it for you. Be prepared." She did a lot of research on the company, realizing quickly that the reason she hadn't found jobs posted is that they recruited directly from colleges. But not the one she had gone to. She knew she needed to understand any exceptions to that rule.

Introducing herself, she said, "Many accounting firms do great work, but I have seen where you go the extra mile. Every year, you have your employees take time to do volunteer work for a local charity. That really inspired me. I'd love to learn more about your company." The informational interview lasted an hour. The man was so inspired by her lead-in that he shared his experiences volunteering, as well as telling her about the company. Before she left, he had arranged two other interviews with managers lower in the organization—people who might be able to hire her. He explained that there were exceptions to the recruiting policy. "When we find really great candidates, like you," he said. Kaneesha felt like dancing out of the meeting.

Not every informational interview will lead to a job, but every interview will lead to a heightened understanding of what the market is looking for, making you a much better candidate in an interview. It also helps to build your confidence in your interviewing skills and will add to your network. When you can't find a job posting, go for the informational interview. Find the jobs that never get posted and land one of them.

> *"Do one thing every day that scares you."*
> *— Eleanor Roosevelt, First Lady*

Summary

Informational interviews are much easier to land than job interviews. And yet, not only do you have the opportunity to learn a great deal about companies of interest. You also have the potential to see these interviews lead to jobs. This is one of the powerful methods of finding all the 'hidden' jobs—the ones that aren't posted.

CHAPTER 13

Interview Preparation

"Success doesn't come to you, you go to it."
— Marva Collins, educator

Many people don't prepare at all for an interview. Beyond cursory research of the company, it is common to believe that you can answer questions about yourself easily. However, in a competitive job market, lack of preparation can keep you from landing a job.

> Indira feared she would be late for her interview. She had the suit her mother picked out and a book to read on the train. But this morning, it took her a long time to get her hair fixed the way she wanted it, and then there were delays on the train. She was flushed and nervous by the time she entered the company headquarters. The receptionist sniffed as she explained how sorry she was to be a little late. "They're waiting for you," she said.

They? She had expected only one interviewer, but the woman clearly had said 'they.' Indira felt even more uneasy. She was late, a little sweaty from her run, and now would be facing a panel.

As she entered the conference room she saw a group of people already seated, leaving a place for her at the end of the table. The women were dressed in designer dresses and looked fashion-forward. The men could have stepped out of GQ. They had tablets open and cups of coffee. *I could really use some coffee,* she thought. But none was offered. Glancing at the clock, she realized she was 10 minutes late. It didn't sound like much, but she felt the tension in the room. And she felt like she had missed the mark with her conservative, dated suit. *I couldn't have chosen worse if I had worn the sari I wore throughout school.*

The group greeted her and she could see they each had a copy of her job application in front of them. When asked for her résumé, she flushed and pulled from her purse a much-folded copy. It hadn't occurred to her that they would ask, as she had attached a .pdf file of it to her job application. As they fired questions at her, making careful notes of her answers, she began to wonder if she should have brought some paper or her tablet. She couldn't even keep track of who was who; the questions just kept coming so fast. Some really threw her. They asked about her worst failure, not about her biggest success. One wanted to know what she thought she'd most like to change about herself. Finally, they asked her if she had any questions. Flustered, she couldn't think of any.

Interviews can be filled with landmines, but careful preparation ensures that you won't miss a great opportunity simply because you weren't prepared. In this chapter and the next, you'll learn what you should be doing before you walk into the room. Most chefs understand that the success of their complex dishes is in the preparation – the *mise en place*. It enables them to put together the finished dish in a short amount of time; diners hate to wait. You need to adopt the same approach so you can deliver your best easily in an interview.

Whether you got the interview through a company communication or through a headhunter (recruiter), it is a fair question to ask who will be doing the interview(s) and to check on the format. Group interviews are a lot less intimidating if you are expecting them. And knowing that you will be speaking with a variety of people helps you prepare for the different kinds of interviews you might face. In most cases, you will speak with the hiring manager, but depending on the position, you may also speak to his or her boss, other peer managers, and members of the hiring manager's team. Each kind of interview has its own challenges. When you know who you will be speaking with and why, you can be better prepared.

First, in this always-connected world, you can look people up. Many have pictures on one of the social media sites. Most managers will be on LinkedIn. Start here and you can learn a lot about the people you will speak with. Make notes about what you learn-past experience, education, interests, etc. You'll learn in the next chapter how to use this information in conversation. Also note if you are LinkedIn with anyone in their network. These are people who might be able to give you some background on the interviewer(s). If no one pops up, just search your network to see if you know anyone at that company. Again, they might give you useful advice about the company and its policies. The more you know about the interview team, the better you will be able to hit the ground running.

Though you may already have done some research on the company, it's time to go back and review it. You want to look at any corporate pictures. You may also find them by typing in the company name in Google Images. You can get hints as to how people dress at work. Your aim is to dress equally to or one step better than what you see in the images. While a suit will always work, if you're uncomfortable in it, consider other ways to look professional. For men, a sports jacket over a nice shirt and khakis may be appropriate in any but the most formal environments or locations. For women, a stylish dress or a skirt with a jacket can take you through a lot of different types of interviews.

If the interview is local, you can walk by the office building as people arrive or leave and check in. Dress is still somewhat important if you are doing a video interview. Just as news people on TV look professional (though we know that some are more casually dressed 'under the desk'), so too should you wear something that on the video will make you look professional. It helps to set the tone.

Go back and look at the job description again. What requirements highlight your strengths? What gives you cause for concern? Prepare to lead with your strengths and explain how other factors (proven quick ability to learn, allied experience or other relevant information) ensures that you are able to measure up to the job.

Make a list of the ten questions you dread hearing most. Prepare answers, but don't memorize them. Work with a friend and become comfortable answering tough questions. When you can keep your cool even when challenged, you can demonstrate to the interviewer that you can work well under pressure. Remember: every aspect of an interview will be considered. How you look, how much you respect their time, your tone, the completeness of your answers, and much more will impact their decision, even if they aren't conscious of all these factors.

Here are some questions to start you off. Practice is essential. Most of us haven't been through a lot of tough interviews and, when you feel confident, you will stand out. Remember, most managers have never really studied interviewing, so they rely on questions they have always felt were good in the past or that they have read in books. They're not out to attack you; these questions are designed to help them know how to hire. But they aren't always worded well. Don't forget to ask for clarification if you don't understand one.

1. What would you consider your biggest failure?
2. What one aspect of your personality would you love to change?
3. What could you be a lot better at?
4. Explain these gaps in your education? Employment history?
5. Why did you leave your last job? Or why are you considering leaving your job?

Strangely, one non-threatening question can actually be the most difficult for some people. "Tell me about yourself." This sounds like an invitation to provide a mini-bio, but it really isn't. You can either have planned a short summary of how you got to the point where you were applying for a job, or you can ask them if they'd prefer a summary of major events in your life or simply a focus on the aspects of your life directly relevant to the job. Though experienced job seekers can really rock the latter choice, when your experience was mostly in after school jobs, it may be difficult to tie it to the current job. Let's see how this might work.

TeShawn knew his track record in fast food wouldn't carry much weight with the insurance company he wanted to work for. But after working through test questions with a friend, he got some insight into how he might be able to spin it more skillfully.

When asked to talk about himself, he began, "As you can see, I've spent most of my college years working for the local pizzeria. Though I really wanted to try for jobs that would give me experience in my future field, most of these were day jobs and I couldn't make them work with my coursework. As you might note, I am looking to move into a career position with a company like yours, but until then, I am still the manager of the pizzeria.

"I worked my way up into this position by demonstrating outstanding sales skills. Of course, I was always on time, dressed and ready and able to do all aspects of the job. But my forté was in upselling. I developed a skill in getting a customer to buy a larger pizza or add more ingredients. For our dine-in customers, I could usually get them to upgrade from a beer to a pitcher and from the lower-end brews to our higher-end microbrews. In promoting me, the shop owner said that he needed someone who understood the value of increasing every sale, while making the customer feel that he was experiencing the attention of someone who cared about his needs."

TeShawn had learned that his employers had a casual dress policy, but he also didn't want to look like he had just run in from his job. The insurance company favored red in their trademark and advertising. He selected a muted red shirt and a pair of tan slacks. He practiced his handshake with his friend, realizing that a fist bump probably wouldn't cut it. Over time, he learned how to use the right amount of pressure and to hold it just the right amount of time. His handshake helped him display his confidence.

He also worked hard on the questions he wanted to ask. By the time they finished, he not only knew much more about how the company worked, he had managed to put in a few comments to indicate how his pizza-selling methods could work with insurance, too.

At the end of the interview, the manager asked him when he could speak to a few other sales managers. TeShawn had to restrain himself from letting out a cheer. The thing that surprised him the most as he left the office was how relaxed he had been and how much he enjoyed speaking with the manager.

The secret to interview preparation is to gather as much information about the company and the people as you can, then work to be clear on how you can be a great employee for them. If you don't know this, they won't know it.

Finally, always bring clean, unfolded copies of your résumé to the meeting. Bring a pad of paper and at least two writing devices. And be on time. First impressions really do count in interviews, even your first impressions of them.

"We don't know where our first impressions come from or precisely what they mean, so we don't always appreciate their fragility."
- Malcolm Gladwell, writer

Summary

Getting an interview is a big win, but if you aren't prepared, you may lose out on a job you really wanted. Take time to prepare and practice for every interview, even if you have been doing them for a while. Learn from each one and keep growing. Practice lands jobs.

CHAPTER 14

Key Secrets of Successful Interviews

> "So many people out there have no idea what they want to do for a living, but they think that by going on job interviews they'll magically figure it out. If you're not sure, that message comes out loud and clear in the interview."
> —TODD BERMONT, WRITER

After public speaking, many people cite tests and interviews as their biggest fears. Job hunting often features all three. You have to do your best speaking (about yourself), interview well, and often prove your abilities through a test. However, the interview part can actually be fun. The fact is that, while most interviewers appear to be engaging in an interrogation (which almost no one enjoys), what an interview should in fact be is a conversation. Too often, advice is given to plan for an interview by learning answers to key, tough questions, as well as bringing some stock questions to ask. This doesn't translate to a conversation. And yet, most of us actually enjoy a friendly conversation.

But how do you do this? First, you want to go in there with a strong understanding of your value. You aren't a supplicant begging for a job and a salary. You are offering your skills, experience and hard work in exchange for a salary. You're equals meeting on a level playing field. Either party may decide that a contract or an agreement isn't possible. Knowing this, you can speak with the interviewing manager just as you would speak to someone you don't know but would like to get to know.

Mario had carefully memorized answers to the tough questions he knew he might hear. He also had a list of questions about the company that were designed to show that he had researched well and knew what he was applying for. Still, from the first moment he sat down, he felt as if he were simply target practice for the manager. The first one stumped him. "Tell me about yourself." Not expecting this, he began a long-winded story about where he was born, grew up and went to school, etc., only belatedly realizing that this couldn't have been what the manager wanted.

After all while, it appeared that the manager simply wanted to test him. The questions were unrelated to the job and so many made him feel stupid. Proud of his degree from a good college, he resented being asked about subjects that had nothing to do with the job. Still, really wanting to get a job, any job, he kept patiently responding while his spirits sagged. He knew he wasn't getting this job.

In the previous chapter, we talked about preparing for interviews. Part of the preparation is remembering how to converse. This doesn't mean answering questions until you're asked if you have any. Instead, you can transform what is a difficult conversation for both parties into a pleasant one simply by using your best first date manners. Finish your answers with a question. Offer information that relates to shared experiences and interests between you and the interviewer. Show genuine interest. While you don't want to dominate the conversation, you also don't want to sit quietly waiting for yet another question. Part of your interview practice should be to learn how to turn the questioning into a conversation.

But there's a caveat. Often, when people get very comfortable, they may forget the etiquette of interviews. Interviews tend to be a play in three acts. Act 1 is where you show what you can bring to the company. You demonstrate your knowledge of the company and the job, highlight where your skills match what they need and show how you can solve present day challenges they mention. Act 2 only comes when there is clear interest. This is where you begin to ask about more details on what your role would be, what a day in the life of a team member would be, etc. Act 3 begins only when you have been offered the job. Only then do you begin to ask about salaries, benefits, career paths, etc. It's all about them in Act 1, a dance between you in Act 2, and about your needs only in Act 3. It's easy to slip into Act 3 prematurely, but avoid the temptation. Until they really want you, talking about what you want in terms of benefits only annoys people.

This leads to the second critical thought. People hire people they like. In this day of diversity, this doesn't mean people like them, but people they can see enjoying working with for a period of time. The hiring manager also has to consider how you would fit into the team. Do you bring not only the skills needed, but a desire to work on a team? Are you conversationally comfortable? Soft skills are increasingly important in the job market and, in a sense, the interview is a test of that. This is why mirroring can help. When you match your pacing, tone of voice, style of speaking, etc., to the interviewer, it helps him to see how you can fit in. By sharing common interests and experiences, the manager will find more ways to like you.

Third, you want to be clear as to what you are looking for and what you can do for them. While most job descriptions are generated by Human Resources and may not really line up with the specific job itself, make sure you understand what they are looking for early in the conversation. Then you can match your abilities to the demands of the job. One of the best techniques to attract interest in an interview is to show how you can solve a problem for a company. Give it away-your efforts will pay off.

Caressa had studied marketing in college. While she knew it might be hard to break in, she had a good deal of experience in social media from fund-raising activities she had done while in college. She asked the interviewer, "What would you say is your biggest challenge in the area of marketing?"

The manager smiled and said, "Twitter. We don't know what we are doing there."

Caressa smiled. "If you'd like, I can show you how I used Twitter to drive people to my fund raising site and then used Tweeting to respond to comments and issues. It's really a powerful platform."

"Tell me more."

Caressa hesitated. She'd be happy to tell her anything if only she had the job. Then she told herself to go for it anyway. "If you don't mind, I've looked at how you are using social. Right now, every Tweet tries to sell, which isn't considered great Twitter etiquette. And when you send them to your site, it's always the home page. Provide links to value-added material, like webinars and white papers. Link to news items and other information people would value from you. And when you send them to your site, send them directly where you want them to go. And you could do a lot more with hash-tags."

The words just tumbled out and Caressa felt a rush of fear. Had she said too much?

The woman smiled at her. "This is exactly what we need. I knew it. All our old-timer marketing execs are lost in this space." Caressa watched as she took careful note of her suggestions.

"Can you come in next week and meet with some of my team? We always like to make sure everyone's good with working with each other."

Caressa nailed it. You can't be too cagey with your knowledge. Giving it away generally pays off well in this situation because it is so rarely done. It's easy to think: "Well, if they want this, they can pay me for it." But consider that most people feel this way. Those few who realize the value of proving their value by giving ideas away are the ones who stand out. They're the ones who get the jobs.

In most conversations, questions arise naturally, but it's always a good idea to be prepared with some questions you really want to ask. These can evoke important information, such as asking a potential peer what a 'day in the life' of their job looks like. But most important are questions that allow you to further emphasize your value to the company. "What is the biggest challenge facing the group today?" This allows you to offer some ideas of how you might help them if you were hired, as demonstrated above. You can also ask them what they consider the most important value/ability/quality that they are seeking in a new hire. These kinds of questions allow you to emphasize how you will be of value to them.

An important recommendation is about telling the truth. It is vital to be honest, though you can slightly accentuate what you do well, but only if you feel confident that you can demonstrate it when needed. The problem with implying that you have experience you lack is that you will shortly be called upon to prove it. While anyone can quickly expand on an existing base of knowledge, it can be tough to simply pick something up from scratch. Instead, if you don't meet all the requirements, talk about what you do well. For example, if the job requires knowing how to use some software that you aren't familiar with, but you do have a lot of experience learning new software, leverage that. Most people understand that if you can learn one program, you can learn any of them. It can be tempting to make yourself sound better than you are, but remember, job specifications are wish lists. In most cases, you don't have to fill all the requirements to be a viable job candidate. Better to be honest and emphasize how quickly you learn, especially if you can cite examples of how quickly you picked up new material. The interviewer will respect that.

When you conclude the initial interview, it is important to understand what happens next. Too often, you're just so glad to be done that you thank them, shake hands and leave. Later, you realize you have no idea how much time it will take to hear from them, if you ever do. Instead, politely ask them what the next steps will be. Do they plan to invite you to interview with other people at the company? How long before you might hear something? Express genuine interest, but try to get some idea of the timeframe.

One killer question that the more audacious candidates may ask is, "Based on what you've learned so far, have you heard anything that would cause you not to offer me the job right now?" Why would you ask? If there are any lingering concerns or issues, you are better off hearing them right then when you might take corrective action. People have used various versions of this question—the exact wording can be your own—but when you can end with this, it ensures that you have left no stones unturned.

After the interview, be sure to send thank-you notes to everyone you have spoken to. Nowadays, email is fine, but make it professional. These emails will be judged. Remind them of high points in the interview, express again your interest in the job and end with some indication that you expect/hope to hear from them soon. You might say, "If you don't mind, I'll email you again in a week to hear how things are progressing." Or remind them of what they said the timeframe and follow-up actions would be. The hiring cycle is much slower now than it has been in the past, and many have found they have not been informed if they didn't get the job. By keeping the lines of communication open, you're more likely to hear.

Remember that the purpose of an interview is to help the interviewer like you enough to present an offer that you would be happy to accept. You are offering value for value. If you don't get this job (or don't want it), you'll have learned more about interviewing, so you can do even better on the next one.

"You have to be unique and different, and shine in your own way."
– Lady Gaga, singer

Summary

When managed in the right way, interviews can be fun. When the interviewer relaxes and begins to enjoy the conversation, you have greatly increased your odds of getting the job. Remember the key points:

- An interview is a conversation. Engage in it as you would with a new person, asking questions and being engaged in a dialogue, not an interrogation.
- Remember your value. This is a negotiation between equals, not a beggar pleading for a job.
- Be clear on what you have to offer and understand how to communicate it effectively.
- In early phases, focus on how you can contribute value to the company. Demonstrate it by giving away solutions if you think of them.
- Be honest. Be prepared to explain anything that might not be positive, but never lie about it.
- Ask about 'next steps'.
- Send thank-yous to everyone.
- Be persistent, but polite.

CHAPTER 15

Closing the Deal

> "I am overly ambitious because I
> realize that it can be done."
> — PHARRELL WILLIAMS, SINGER

You'll know that the interviewer is interested when they begin to ask more about what you want than what you can do for them. As some time may intervene between interview cycles, always be in touch with the company to understand what else they might need from you and to remind them of highlights from your interview. If you get an additional idea of something that might work for them, tell them. You're seeking to differentiate yourself from the other candidates. Assume that you might all be essentially qualified for the position. You'll get the offers because of those elements that set you apart from the competition.

Naomi had several summer positions doing support functions for an office. Having worked full-time while going to college, she was a master at figuring out the most efficient ways to work. During interviews at a large bank, the interviewer explained how many complex processes each person had to learn. As the interviews took place at the headquarters office, she overheard people constantly asking each other how to do something. No one seemed to have any documentation or 'getting started' guides. Remembering that, in her follow-up discussions and emails with the bank, she offered the idea that she could create a manual that documented frequently-executed procedures so that anyone coming in could quickly come up to speed and work proficiently.

Her note was almost an afterthought, but she remembered that they had seemed interested in some of her ideas during the interview. A few days later, she received a call offering her the job.

Assess what they are looking for and what makes you special. Emphasize this, especially in your notes and calls to them. You want to be remembered. Today, many postings get thousands of applicants. They may interview 50. It's hard to remember everyone you speak with, so set out to make an impression that helps them pick you.

Early on, you need to consider what you care about most in the job offer. One trap is simply to be so glad they are offering a job that you don't want to see if you can get more. In major negotiations, whether you are buying a house or a car, the price is rarely the price. The same is true for jobs. However, your negotiation space is only as large as your value to them. In a tight market, there is a tendency to offer you the lowest salary possible. You can research salaries in your area online (see Resources) to understand the ranges possible. If this is your first career position, you might end up accepting the offer as is, but in general, if everything is going well, no one ever lost the job by asking if they could do a little better.

Other negotiating points might include relocation money, location of work, and vacation or other benefits. Especially if you are fortunate enough to have more than one offer, you want to know more of the details of these benefits. In particular, vacation and medical benefits can vary widely from company to company. You want to make a prudent decision that will net you the best overall package.

Ganesh had family obligations that made working from home a huge advantage. Based on the advice of friends, he didn't go into interviews talking about it, but he knew that jobs in his field, programming, often permitted working remotely. A few major companies in the Silicon Valley had already made it clear that you had to work in the office. He didn't apply to those; it was a long way from his home and he knew he couldn't manage the care his mother needed with a long commute.

When one company indicated interest, a company he had already felt matched his own goals, he weighed the offer carefully. He felt sure that the offer was a little low, but considered that perhaps that gave him an opening to ask to work from home. He said, "That is a little less than I was hoping for. Perhaps it would work if I could work primarily from home." Because he had prioritized his desires upfront, it was easier for the company to accommodate him. They likely wouldn't have offered more money as well as the work-from-home option.

While some companies advertise jobs as work-from-home, many don't let you know upfront. Larger firms may have multiple sites. As you get into the negotiating phase (Act 3), these are the questions you need to ask. If you have to move to take the job, ask about a relocation package. While these are mostly offered to people in higher level positions, it isn't unheard of to offer them to a desirable candidate. But you have to ask. If that isn't an option, consider asking instead for a signing bonus which will help you pay for the move. See what they can do to meet your needs. Once you've proven that you are someone they want, most reasonable requests can be considered. But you can't ask for everything. Consider what matters most.

Health benefits are less variable than they were, but the prices still can be. In some cases, you may not have much choice in insurance companies. More choice is better. The optimal is to be able to select from a variety of plans which might include a plan with low deductibles but higher costs, a plan with higher deductibles and lower cost and one that has a limited network of doctors, but a lower cost. Then you can select the one that fits your situation best. If you have a spouse or dependents, make sure to understand the cost of the coverage and whether or not they will be covered. Some companies have dropped this altogether, and others ask you to pay the entire premium. Today, the cost of insurance is high enough that this can significantly impact the value of the offer. If you only have one offer, you probably can't get them to do anything here. But if you have several, compare the plans. HR should have a sheet they can send you outlining what they offer.

Vacation is the one area that many wish would be more flexible, but too often isn't. But again, it doesn't hurt to ask if you could take several unpaid days per year in addition to your normal vacation. A company may offer 'paid time off' instead of vacation. This means that you earn days each month you work that can be used for sick leave or vacation. You want to understand how your paid time off is calculated and when you can begin to take it.

Some companies offer what they call a 'cafeteria' benefit plan which may include ways you can get extra time off. Never lead with this; you don't want them to think that you can't wait to get away from your new job. But it is on the minds of many people, so if this matters to you, definitely broach the subject.

One new way you can be offered a job is contract for hire. Once rarely considered, many companies are using this as an option this because it gives them an easy out if the hire doesn't work out. Though it may not seem like it given the large numbers of layoffs you hear about, getting rid of people isn't all that easy. Contract for hire is a good way for new workers to start. You know you can prove your value. Just be sure the contract term is reasonable and that you understand the conditions under which you would be offered a permanent job.

Remember not to be too grateful that you were offered a job. You are offering value equal to the offer, so you have a right to weigh the offer and make a counter-proposal. As you go through your career, you will find that learning how to ask for what you want will make a substantial difference in your lifetime earnings. Your biggest salary bumps tend to be as you move from job to job, not from raises or promotions.

"Our choices in life are made according to our sense of our own worth."
– Kaylan Pickford, actress

Summary

Be prepared with what you expect and need from a job offer. Once they are really interested in you, there will be negotiation room. Figure out your 'must haves' before you go into the discussion, but be realistic.

CHAPTER 16

Paperwork

"No job is over until the paperwork is done."
— Anonymous

When you get the job, you should receive a written offer. This way, you will be able to understand your rights and the offer clearly. People can dispute that you heard something, but they can't argue with paper. Even if it is an email offer, you should have something in writing. The next and biggest aspect is the HR paperwork. Depending on the company, it can be substantial. Looking at the stack, you may be tempted to do what you do when you get one of those frequent Apple updates with a legal disclosure to sign. Does anyone really read these? But this is one place where you should take the time. You never know what you will find. In some cases, ignorance can cost you your career.

Liam couldn't believe his luck. He had gotten an offer for the job he had dreamed about. The location was perfect; he had wanted to work in New York. It was where everything was happening. His hometown of Ames, Iowa, had zero nightlife. He knew he'd never be a farmer. The company offered him a relocation package and it included a 'look-see' trip to sign the paperwork and begin to find a place to live.

The sight of the tall buildings struck him speechless. Sure, he'd seen it all on TV and in movies, but it wasn't the same as being there. The energy of the city captured him. He couldn't wait to get started. Encouraged by his new boss, he tore through the paperwork so he could get out on the street and begin to explore.

Four months later, Liam had figured out a few things. The law firm he had joined expected 100 hours per week or more. It was grueling work, none of it the kind of law he had struggled through law school to do. They wanted to groom him for real estate law; he wanted a chance to do trial work. He liked New York, but not as much as he thought he would.

Just as despair, lack of sleep and brain fog threatened to bring him down, his father sent him an email describing a new branch of a national firm opening up in Des Moines. They knew he had done well in mock trial work and wanted to speak with him. Des Moines wasn't New York City, but he found himself longing for the endless vistas. Central Park couldn't replace the corn fields. Never expecting that he would get so excited about his state, he rushed off his résumé with a cover letter. Feigning illness, Liam rushed back for the interview and excited about the offer, took the job.

He returned to New York, told his roommates he was leaving and then penned his letter of resignation. His boss barely responded to it. Others teased him, "We knew you didn't have what it took, farm boy." When he responded to a request from HR for an exit interview, he had no idea what awaited him.

"You realize your relocation money was predicated on your continued employment for at least a year," the HR rep explained. "And we'll need to see which firm you are going to. You signed a non-compete document. If we feel the firm is a competitor, you will be enjoined from working for them for two years."

Liam couldn't believe what he was hearing. The HR rep showed him all the points he had so casually ignored as he signed up. As it turned out, his new firm was on the list of competitors. He had to turn the offer down. Sadly, he suggested that he might stay on.

"I'm sorry," she said. "All resignations are final. Good luck with your career."

Though a dramatic story, this happens every day. In fact, the non-compete clause, though not valid in every state or country, often applies even if you are laid off. Talk about bad luck attracting more bad luck. Liam hadn't looked at any of the documents except the first page of the contract indicating his salary. That blinded him to all other issues.

Read the paperwork. It's a good idea whenever presented a stack of legal papers, because anything binding can include nasty surprises. People have celebrated the purchase of a house only to find that they have a significant pre-payment penalty. If you decide to switch cell phone plans, you may have discovered that there is a cost to do so. Your career is too important to simply trust that the employer has your best interest at heart.

While no company is trying to hurt their employees, they also want to protect themselves. In many cases, HR may not know of some of the details agreed to in a verbal offer. If you negotiated certain benefits, make sure they are in the contract. If you don't understand something, ask. Legal terminology can be confusing. You have a right to understand every line of every page before you sign.

> Eliza's mother warned her to read every page of her contract. As she went through the document—a contract to work for an software company—she found references to a health club and equipment. It didn't seem to relate to anything she would be doing. When you asked, the abashed HR rep replied, "You know, we've used that contract for 10 years. No one has ever mentioned this. I'm guessing someone copied a contract and forgot to change it."

This case, though real, is an extreme example. The former case is far more likely. Some companies ask you to sign mandatory deduction forms for things such as political action committees (PACS) or for a favored charity. The health plan may not be as initially described. You particularly want to watch for what happens if you leave in less than a year, whether by choice or not. Question what looks wrong to you. Often, reasonable requests can result in changes to the contract. These will be only for you, not for others who were less careful.

One noted transit agency requires prospective employees to be unemployed when they enter a training program. They must pay for their training in the hope of landing one of the few openings. There are a variety of 'gotchas', and you need to know what you are willing to give up and what you are willing to do.

One increasingly important issue is privacy rights. Companies have the right to view everything you do on company equipment, such as PCs and phones. Some companies also demand the right to search your desk. If these areas concern you, make sure to get an explanation of what is covered. Can they look in your purse or wallet? At companies producing items of value, you may have to change clothing and be observed while changing. While necessary in some cases, some companies simply have these rights on the contract in case they need them. You can always ask for an explanation and, if the requirement is too onerous, for an exception. However, there is no guarantee that the exception will be granted.

It is important to understand that a contract is a legal document and, by your signature, you are agreeing to all of it. Though you may go your whole career without having to hire an attorney, if you ever find yourself in a bad employment situation, your clear understanding of your contract will be critical. In the most egregious cases, you may find yourself deciding to turn down a job offer. Make sure they understand why. Again, changes are possible, but only before you sign.

It can be helpful to know before you sign. Nolo Press, a service offering legal information at a reasonable cost, offers a book entitled, **"Your Rights in the Workplace."** Consult Resources for other information as to what you might expect.

Take the time to understand what you are signing. You only have one chance to get this right on each job.

Summary

In your delight at landing a job, don't forget to read carefully every document you sign. In some cases, specific line items can be challenged, but if you never read the contract, you won't know what you've agreed to. This is true whether you are signing an employment contract, a lease, or any other legal document. Take the time and take it seriously.

Keeping
Your Job

CHAPTER 17

Hit the Ground Running

> "Start where you are. Use what
> you have. Do what you can."
> — ARTHUR ASHE, ATHLETE

In some ways, the first day on a new job is the easiest. You're generally going through company policies and procedures, meeting colleagues, getting hooked up with equipment and learning about available resources. While this process may span several days, understand that the first six months, including this period, set the tone of your career with this company. You are remembered by how you begin. And you only have a short period of time to be "the new kid on the block." At the end of every day, make sure you can list what you have done and what you learned.

Miguel felt a huge sense of relief when he landed his first career job. His first day made him feel relaxed and happy at his new company. His new team took him to lunch and people kept stopping by to say hi and asking him how he was doing. He spent a fair amount of time exploring the internal website, looking through the engineering resources and learning how to use the CAD/CAM software. He attended meetings, listening closely, hoping to learn as much as possible. Two weeks in, his manager came and asked him how he liked things so far.

"But we're just wondering. When are you going to start showing us why we hired you?"

Miguel felt his stomach clench. *What did he expect?*

"I thought by now you would be trying to get onto projects, asking for work...something like that."

Miguel realized he had been waiting for an assignment, hesitant to push himself forward. Apparently, he had misunderstood the expectation. Now, he had to scramble to change this first impression.

Coming off of summer or after-school jobs, you may be used to receiving specific training and then assignments for work. If this process doesn't happen quickly and you spend weeks doing very little, that's not a problem. It's up to the employer to define your work responsibilities and ensure that you get the training and guidance you need. In career jobs, there is an expectation that new employees will be a bit more assertive. It's a chance not only to show your abilities but also your passion for the job. Being passive isn't a good idea.

But at the same time, you want to watch and listen to understand how people work together and how things get done.

You'll begin to hear about projects and meetings; it gives you a chance to ask if you can listen in or help. People will form an opinion of you within the first three months. It isn't called a probation period simply because Human Resources has a definition for it. For each member of your new team and for your boss, this is when they assess who has been added to the team. People who start off strong begin a career in a far more favorable position. But how do you do this?

First, take as little time to get set up as possible. You can browse the company intranet later. Focus on getting some work to do early on. Volunteer. It doesn't matter if you can't do everything; it only matters that you do something.

> Fran felt very lost after the initial rush of starting the job. Everyone around had something to do but her. There were meetings and tasks to complete and projects, but no one asked her for help. Then she remembered that her manager had brought up a problem they were having on the intranet, a problem she had suggested she could solve.
>
> After speaking with the team lead and getting access to the backend web files, she began to design a better way that people could share information securely on the site. Fran created subgroups with different privileges and set up automatic linkages so that, as you joined a group, you had permission to share, edit and delete files. After showing off her work in a staff meeting, she quickly found herself being given work to do and being invited to meetings. By the end of her first month, she felt like she belonged. And more important, her team felt she belonged, too.

If you have that insight from your interview, start with that project. Ask your new manager or team leader what you can work on. Don't wait for them to ask you. If you hear someone having a challenge or even simply needing bodies to do something, put up your hand. Remember, the team worked effectively before you came along and you need to make your place on that team. Otherwise, they'll rely on the people they always turned to before you arrived.

Even if it is suggested you take your time, be gently insistent on having a chance to show your value and to contribute. The goal is to become the go-to person, the one everyone wants on their project. Might this mean you will be overloaded? It's possible, but you'll learn that much faster. Being new, you will have more latitude when you make a mistake or need to ask a lot of questions. A year from now, you'll be expected to perform at a higher level. If you're not involved early on, you'll miss that valuable, yet cushioned learning opportunity.

Make careful notes on all processes and procedures you learn. Some may be things you only do occasionally. You'll look like a star when no one has to tell you again how to do them. In fact, many new hires have made a difference by creating an informal manual on how to start off successfully at their company. The notes you take are just the ones many people would need as they begin. It's a great strategy that sets you apart at an early phase of your career. Besides, having that manual will save you over and over again. Few people document; be the one who does. It will also help you when you have your performance review.

Ask for feedback at regular intervals, though not daily. Make course corrections as you learn the processes, procedures and culture of your new company. Ask people to lunch; don't just wait to be asked. What you can learn over sandwiches is the kind of insider information that you won't be offered formally.

In gatherings and meetings, don't be afraid to offer your ideas, but note how other people interact and follow their lead. Even if your early ideas aren't adopted–they may, in fact, be impractical in that situation or ones that have already been tried–the team will appreciate that you are offering them. Offer them humbly, being aware that they might not be new.

Be generous and specific in thanking people for helping you. Share success. Be humble. Each of these behaviors will add to your stature even though it might seem at first that you are letting other people shine. People love those who share the credit. But don't give all the credit away. Your best is worth celebrating.

When you speak with people, even if they don't mirror this behavior, gift them with your full attention. Most people don't listen fully. You can differentiate yourself this way. And be kind to yourself. This is a new career, a new job, and mistakes are inevitable. Learn from them and move on.

"Everyone has highs and lows that they have to learn from, but every morning I start off with a good head on my shoulders, saying to myself, 'It's going to be a good day!'"
– Lindsay Lohan, actress

Summary

The best way to launch your career in a new job is to start off fast. Ask for work, learn quickly, and make a contribution as soon as possible. Ask for feedback so you can be sure you are hitting or exceeding the mark. Under-promise and over-achieve. And document what you are learning. It can be overwhelming in the first few months, but the more you write down what you learn, the less you will have to ask for help the next time.

And learn the value of listening with your full attention. It's the best gift you can give anyone.

CHAPTER 18

Teaming With Your Manager

> "I am a member of the team, and I rely on the team, I defer to it and sacrifice for it, because the team, not the individual, is the ultimate champion."
>
> MIA HAMM, ATHLETE

Many view their manager as the task-master, someone you must be careful around. This individual has the power to hire and fire, promote or stall your career, and give or withhold bonuses and raises. But that's really the wrong way to look at it. Though he or she has all those powers, they also can be a guide, a mentor, a trainer and an inspiration. The way it generally works in a company is that your manager is judged on how well the team under them succeeds. As they are rewarded, they will reward you.

We often find ourselves getting caught up in the words "individual contributor," focusing heavily on the individual part. We see ourselves as solo players, bringing our great expertise to the job. It's all about us. But if we don't align with or even understand our manager's goals, we will fail. No one needs to befriend the boss. You do need to be seen by him as an ally and a team player. Each time you get a new manager, you need to learn what he needs and likes from his people. Your number one job is to make him look successful. Don't forget that your company promoted him to this position because they believed in him. Even if you strongly believe that they have made a horrible mistake, you only have two good options: support him fully or move on. You can't shine if you try to stand out as a hero. Even top-gun pilots are part of a larger mission. They don't win points for dropping bombs on targets they find interesting. They need to stay on mission.

After you've had a few jobs, you'll run into a manager who doesn't 'get' you or doesn't appreciate you as much as you think you deserve. After reorganization, you may find that the new boss doesn't value you as much as the previous boss and it's easy to blame him for the problem. After all, the last boss liked and valued you, so it must be him or her. The thing you need to understand is that it doesn't matter if you don't like your boss; you still must please him and align yourself with his goals.

Dexter simply felt relief when he finally found a career job after looking for nearly a year. Desperate to start paying off college loans and earning enough to move away from home; he jumped at the first offer. He hadn't really felt a connection with the manager, and some of his future teammates had mentioned that the man was a bit of a micro-manager, but he ignored his instinct in favor of getting the job.

While other members of the group had adapted and learned how to deal with this manager's style, Dexter felt rebellious and angry about it. He complained several times to HR, believing that they were on his side. After a while, he found himself in a meeting with his manager and HR.

"We understand that there are problems between you," the HR rep said. "Let's talk about this."

Encouraged, Dexter again began to lay out his complaints. A bit worked up, he didn't notice the expressions on the faces of the others.

"I think we've heard what we need to hear," she said.

The manager cleared his throat. "It's clear that this arrangement isn't working out. Since you are in the first 90 days of your employment with us-your probation period-we're going to let you go."

Dexter walked out of the meeting in shock. How had he missed what was really happening?

What could Dexter have done differently, given the mismatch in personalities? How can you cope effectively? Mismatches happen and so do reorganizations. It's very likely that during your tenure with a company, you'll have more than one manager. You'll generally only have some discretion with the first one; you can choose not to take the job.

The first thing is to learn from your mistakes and from those of your friends. You don't have to love your boss, but you have to find one you can work with. Part of your interview conversation has to be about understanding him or her well enough to see if you can work with their style. You can also ask your future teammates. Ask them what they like and don't like about working with the manager.

But, as noted, you will have other managers because change is inevitable. What do you do when the company reorganizes and you feel some discomfort about the change in leadership? The first thing is to put yourself in the new manager's shoes. You're taking over a group that apparently functioned fine. How do you start off without knowing what is going on?

Ruth had worked hard and finally earned a promotion to management. Her boss felt she had done such a good job turning around projects that he gave her a team that needed some real guidance. In the last year, this team's ability to get problems resolved had slowed and customers were complaining. He wanted her to fix it.

Ruth was scared. She had only been at the company two years and this had been her first real job. She loved that her boss believed in her, but she also worried that her skills weren't up to the task. She spent the weekend trying to work out what to say to her new team.

On Monday, she called a staff meeting and let them know that they were to move towards a better customer experience, which meant being more responsive and learning to listen well. She worded it gently and didn't call out problems from the past, hoping to be liked. In the first few moments, she could tell that most of her team had liked things just the way they were.

But one person had a different perspective; he understood his "number one job." Ben's father had told him that his real job was to make his boss look good. He saw the reaction of the others and thought he might be able to do just that.

Ben asked for a meeting with Ruth, offering to show her what he had been working on. He asked her how she would like him to move up to the new program. In the conversation, he continually prodded her to explain in detail what he should be doing to help her achieve the new goals. In addition, he asked if they might have biweekly meetings to check on his progress.

Ruth sighed with relief when he left. She scheduled similar meetings with every other team member and the results began to show up. Aware of how much Ben's outreach had helped her, she quickly moved him to a team lead position.

In the past, it may have seemed that excellent work from a contributor should shine on its own. Isn't that fair? Shouldn't your best efforts be recognized? Again, we look at other situations where being a solo star isn't productive. Everyone really needs a team. Bicycle racing is a perfect example. No cycling star ever made it without the expert support of their team. All team sports work the same way, but even sports such as car racing require an excellent team. Front-men for musical groups also rely on their 'teams' to make them look great. While your individual work must be excellent, it has to be in the service of the team and company goals or it won't really matter to your career.

Individual contributors need to remember that their "contribution" needs to align with company goals. Even as you rise in a company, you still have to get clarity as to what your management team-and most importantly your manager-needs from you.

Everyone will step into this particular career 'hole' at some point. It's impossible to like everyone, and it's also impossible to always understand what is wanted from someone who is very unlike you. There are ways to handle this more effectively. The points to remember are:

1. Your manager isn't your pal. This means that you aren't expected to like or befriend your boss. Just as it is with team sports, you simply need to work together. Your quarterback will call the plays, and you need to understand them and support them.
2. Learn what your manager wants and needs. First, you need to understand the priorities and work product expected. That's the basics. Getting to a good place with your manager goes beyond that. You need to understand their personal style. Typically, if you don't get along, you do not share that style. There are techniques, such as Social Styles[2], which can help you learn strategies to work with others, discover their needs, and then deliver on them. See below for an example.
3. Meet frequently with your manager for a quick checkpoint. Don't wait until issues arise. Proactively share your progress and find out how you're doing. This allows for quick course corrections. Set up a short meeting every week or every other week, understanding that business priorities may lead meetings to be cancelled.

2 http://socialstyles360.com/

4. Share your status in writing, even if the manager doesn't ask for this. Keep a copy on file.
5. Ask questions to gain more information, not to make you look smart.
6. Develop your listening skills.

Rashid had studied psychology in college and in his classes had learned that, when interacting with others, it made sense to not assume that everyone reacted the same way to a given situation. In a stress situation, he had learned to find his calm center and became very analytical, which was helpful in rapidly resolving the difficult problems he encountered.

He realized that Moises, his manager, did not have the same reaction. Problems made him feel stressed. When someone rushed in with a crisis, Moises reacted strongly. It took time for him to get to a place where he could carefully consider the situation. By recognizing their differences, Rashid tried something new when he had to bring a problem to Moises. Instead of rushing in with the details, he started with a friendly comment, often referring to a sporting event from the previous night. They both enjoyed watching sports on TV.

After a few minutes, he calmly mentioned the problem, sharing his ideas of how to solve it. He asked Moises for input and permission. Having settled the issue, he ended the conversation with a few more friendly words.

Moises reacted completely differently with this approach. Instead of panicking and raising his voice, Rashid could see that Moises worked more effectively when he wasn't challenged. Over time, it became clear that Rashid stood out as a star; Moises felt that Rashid simply had fewer problems than other team members. Rashid understood how important it was to adapt to his manager's style to achieve the desired results.

In reality, not every manager you have will be a great one. Ask anyone. We all remember the bad managers we've had, even more than the good ones. But you can't always hope to have a great one. Even if you don't feel great about your working relationship, if you align with your manager's goals and keep delivering cheerfully, you will be much more likely to be able to make a move.

Be a success by making your manager a success. It's easier than you think.

Summary

Your number one job is to support your manager in achieving his goals and those of his company. Do this, and you will shine as an individual.

CHAPTER 19

Managing the Age Gap

"Each generation imagines itself to be more intelligent than the one that went before it, and wiser than the one that comes after it."

GEORGE ORWELL, WRITER

When working in the kinds of jobs you had in high school and college, most of your colleagues were probably around your age. The manager might be older (or not), but day-to-day, you would be working with people of your own generation. Career jobs will confront you with people from a wide variety of generations. While it might be nice to simply say that 'people are people,' in fact, when you were born and what happened as you grew up has a profound effect on who you are now. Those who grew up during World War II have a different view of America and the world than those who were young adults during the Viet Nam war.

As people live and work longer, the workplace now comprises at least four generations (and sometimes five), all with their own worldviews. Known by various names and with date ranges varying slightly, who you will meet will be:

- Silent Generation – 1900-1945 (smallest number left)
- Baby Boomers – 1946-1964
- Gen X – 1965-1980
- Gen Y (Millennials) – 1981-1999
- Gen Z – 2000-present

The two most challenging mistakes people make in dealing with those of different generations are either assuming that everyone is just like them or holding narrow assumptions about the generational differences. Yet, the differences in values, lifestyles and attitudes can cause friction if they aren't understood and embraced.

As a Millennial, Risa had been born into a technologically-enabled world where it appeared anything was possible. The fast rate of progress made her feel that she could advance rapidly. Having been writing code since she was a child, she felt she could quickly move to a senior position at the software company where she worked. As part of her interview, she had demonstrated several apps she had written, all of which were popular on iTunes and other download sites.

Risa's manager, a Baby Boomer, had launched his career on the mainframe and frankly felt smart phones and tablets were an unavoidable nuisance. He realized that all development had to run on these platforms, but gave more of the interesting work to his senior (and older) developers. As Risa had no experience on mainframes or UNIX, he didn't offer her the respect she felt she had earned. She found herself arguing with him nearly every day about how to approach a problem, what she should be working on, and even how she should be valued.

As the arguments continued, Risa found herself telling her colleagues that the manager should retire. "He's old enough, certainly," she said. Word got back to him and the situation became even more difficult.

Risa deserved respect for her experience, but at almost every company you pay your dues and earn respect by accomplishing simpler, smaller tasks first. She didn't see the need to do that and hated the term 'pay your dues.' Nor did she accord her manager any respect and her age-biased comments could lead to disciplinary action. She didn't value the experience he had and he could tell. At the same time, because she didn't feel a need to prove herself, her manager fell back on people he could communicate with. He didn't 'get' her and she didn't 'get' him.

A basic rule about human interaction is that we can't really change anyone but ourselves. It's a hard truth, but truth it is. In workplace generational conflicts, it is on you to figure out how to work with the other person by understanding who they are and gently helping them understand who you are. By adapting and understanding, you are more likely to encourage that behavior from others. Reach your hand out first and you'll find more hands reaching towards you.

Let's look at the generations a little so we can try to understand where they are coming from. Realize that these are generalizations and that there are exceptions to everything.

- **Silent Generation** – Many are past the age where we would have expected them to retire. They are still working either because they love their jobs or because they have to for financial reasons. They grew up when you typically worked at the same job all your life, hard work was rewarded, and loyalty was a two-way street. More conservative, they question authority much less than other generations and are suspicious of those who do. They like the status quo and may resist change, but offer significant wisdom and historical perspective.
- **Baby Boomers** – Along with Millennials, these are the most numerous generation; they represent a generation of hope after World War II. Work ethic is a core value, and you will see them expect to work long hours of overtime but expect the rewards to follow. Unlike their forefathers, they constantly challenge the status quo. For many, success equals advancement, so those who haven't achieved a management role may feel they have failed. Though competent users of the latest technology, they don't feel the same comfort level later generations do. Baby Boomers also have a lot of experience and perspective to share. Many are willing and happy to be mentors.
- **Gen X** – This generation grew up with technology and may not know a world without computers and the Internet. This translates to an easy facility with new software and tech; helping others struggling with technology is a great way to make a mark. With the rapid rate of change in society, social values and conditions, this generation may be more comfortable with change.

As such, they are more likely than previous generations to change jobs and even careers many times during their lives. Highly focused, many will advance faster and farther than any generation before.

- **Gen Y** (Millennials) – The next 'Boomer' wave, this generation includes many who are still in school and too many who are seeking jobs and finding the market much tougher than they expected. Children of the Baby Boomers, they believe in their ability to effect change and make the world what they want. Equally comfortable with technology, they can also differentiate themselves by helping older workers get comfortable with technological change.

When we look for friends, we start by looking for people who have things in common with us and those who have something of value to offer. This approach can help in the workplace. Look at what each generation can offer to help you with your career. All have value; all have something special. But go further. You may be surprised to learn that your oldest colleague also enjoys some of the same sports you do. They may share a love for certain TV shows, books you love or other hobbies. You may have attended the same schools. When you find connections, it is easier to appreciate another person. Focus on the commonalities, not the differences and relationship building will be easier.

Figure out ways in which the differences can help you. We're all exposed to the concept that diversity per se is valuable. Well, generational diversity is another aspect of the diversity picture. If each generation operated this way, there would be no 'generation gap.' However, one person can make a huge difference simply reaching out to others.

Here is some basic advice for working with anyone, but particularly for people of different generations.

- Be respectful. Everyone deserves respect.
- Give your full attention to them. The best gift you can give anyone is to really listen to them. This means giving good eye contact and not multi-tasking.
- Don't make assumptions. We've all known people from a variety of generations, but there is no typical representative. Let everyone be themselves, not their generation.

If you are young and working with older individuals, a few tips can help:

- Choose face-to-face conversations. This makes it personal to them. While comfortable with some degree of virtual presence, most of the older generation grew up before email.
- Be patient. People from different generations have different perspectives and even different language. If you lead with patience, they will respond that way to you.
- Focus on what you can get from these interactions. Older workers have more experience with the inevitable politics, the 'way things are done here' and organizational codes. You can save a ton of time learning from them.

- Ask questions, but do your own research as well. People respect those who have 'done their homework' and are far more likely to help when they see the effort.
- Find at least one to be your mentor. If your goal is to move quicker than the organization expects new hires to move, a mentor will be an essential aid in this pursuit.

If you are older and working with Gen X or Y, you can also achieve better results with a few tips:

- Start with the idea that these generations have a great deal to offer. Condescension will only hurt the relationship.
- Be clear. Corporate jargon will be new to them and you can help them learn it, but it's not how you begin.
- Speak to them thru Skype, email and texting, if you possibly can. Reach across the divide and take your game to the next level.
- Give the new people the chance to work on their own and learn by trying and making mistakes. It's how everyone learns.
- Relax. This can actually be fun.

Nadine followed in her father's footsteps and signed up to learn to be a mainframe programmer. He warned her, "Some of us are old, crusty types and hard to get to know. Just be patient." But she wasn't. She had created several great programs in her last year and was sure she could do a great job. Still, her father had never steered her wrong.

The first day, she found one quiet man who seemed open to speaking with her. He became her mentor and showed her where to copy JCL when she needed to create something. He gave her a cheat sheet on acronyms and basically, walked her through her first assignment. Their relationship caused everyone else to relax. To her surprise, she found that the initial reservation she felt from others had more to do with their fear of being laid off than because they were afraid new people in the field could displace them. Nadine felt sympathetic to their fears. She remembered being the 'new kid on the block' in her summer jobs and being the first fired.

She listened, a lot, and discovered that while her team was expert on the mainframe, many of them struggled to make the company-supplied smart phones work well. Offering help, she quickly became seen as a valuable asset and a go-to person for modern tech.

In just a few months, she felt comfortable and happy working with what had become a team of fathers anxious to see her succeed.

"If I were given the opportunity to present a gift to the next generation, it would be the ability for each individual to learn to laugh at himself."
Charles M. Schulz, cartoonist

Summary

Friction is inevitable when different types of people collide, but there are ways to minimize it and achieve quick wins by being the person everyone likes to have around. By understanding not just your generation, but the others you work with, you can bridge the gap. It only takes one person to make a huge difference in the office climate.

CHAPTER 20

The Power of WIIFM

> "Before you judge my life, my past or my
> character, walk in my shoes, walk the
> path I have traveled, live my sorrow, my
> doubts, my fear, my pain and my laughter.
> Remember everyone has a story."
> SUSHAN R. SHARMA, ALIAS & UNKNOWN SOURCE

When you have to negotiate with someone or get an agreement, it can help to remember these words. We begin our dialogue by thinking of what we hope to gain from the conversation, when what we need to do is think about what the other person wants and understand their story. WIIFM means "what's in it for me." It's so easy, when we seek help or seek to persuade, to be narrowly focused on what **we** need or want. We begin by planning how to convince someone, but, without understanding their position, this approach is rarely as successful as you might like. Jokes have been made about the case of the young man applying for a job. When asked why he should be selected, he responds, "Because I need the money." It sounds obvious how unpersuasive this would be, but how many of us remember asking for a raise in our allowance with no better argument than that?

There is a basic rule: people tend to do what is in their own best interest. If we don't understand this fact of human nature, we will be less successful in our interactions. When applying for a job, too many focus on what they want from the job, not on what they can contribute. You might say that you want a chance to design gaming software, or to learn more about the practical application of your economics degree. These goals are important, but they do not close the deal. They're about you, not the person you're trying to persuade.

WIIFM is about the fundamental golden rule: in most situations, we do things that serve our interests in some way. When you ask for help, you need to understand that the person you are asking is considering how your request can serve them. This means that part of the job is trying to understand the needs and desires of the other party. When you can't figure that out and you don't play to it, often you won't get what you want. Has this happened to you?

When you want to influence someone or ask for a favor or for a job, you must understand what they might want and how you can deliver on that. How can helping you help them? Some people seem to simply get it. We've all known that person everyone wants to help, the one who can persuade. How do they do it? It isn't a gene for luck. Simply, it's the power of understanding the power of WIIFM.

Sean had gotten summer and after-school jobs easily because his father had loads of contacts. After college, he began to look for a career job in his field, electrical engineering. While he knew an advanced degree might help, he didn't have the money to continue. In each interview, he felt he had shown a lot of enthusiasm for the company and the position, but he never got called back. He couldn't figure it out. He had done really well in school and really needed the job.

His best friend, JJ, landed a job a month after graduating. Sean first wrote it off to luck, but as time went on, he thought he might ask JJ for some help. JJ did have a secret—knowing how to use WIIFM. "When I go into an interview, I've already talked to a few people who work for the company. I've tried to understand the problems they have and come up with how my skills could help them solve those problems. That's what we talk about." JJ led with why a company would want to hire him; Sean focused only on why he wanted the job. One method simply has a higher success rate than the other.

Although you can't literally 'walk a mile in their shoes,' your goal is to get some understanding of their needs and challenges by putting yourself in their place. A manager hiring a new employee wants someone who will quickly be productive, work well with the existing team, and be happy to learn. It's very easy to just go back to what you know best (your needs), but that's like buying a gift for a friend that is something you want, without considering what they like. Good friends know about this. They own their own desires and don't assume the other person shares them. When selecting a restaurant or a movie to go to, each person is thinking of the likes and dislikes of their friend, so that the end result pleases both. And when it's something only you want, you learn to convey it in a way that makes the other person more willing to agree. You give them some stake in the outcome.

Kyla really wanted her best friend, Mae, to join her on a trip to Hawaii; it would be their first time out of the continental U.S. She couldn't wait to try to surf and zip-line; there were so many activities to try. But Mae was a spa-girl. She liked luxury and relaxation. She didn't want to invest her hard-earned vacation money in an athletic holiday.

Considering this, Kyla started searching sites in Hawaii aimed at the more sedentary kind of vacation. She quickly realized that between sunbathing and spa-hopping, Mae could have fun too. Selling first the idea of the relaxing vacation, Kyla was able to get Mae on board. In the end, both of them shared in a lot of events, enjoying seeing what the other one liked to do.

The 'rewards', the WIIFM, are as individual as the person, and can be immediate or longer range. Though our society tends to think in terms of tangible rewards... things... successful WIIFM-masters understand the power of the intangible. You don't have to be a trained psychologist; the key is curiosity. Kyla knew her friend really well, so she could imagine what she wanted. But it never hurts to ask.

Team sports work this way. When a player wants to be considered for a new position on the team, he has to convince his coach or manager that he will be an asset to the team in that position. He also needs to reassure him that the team will not lose out when he makes the move.

When learning to understand what others want, use this process:

1. Remember that it isn't about what you want or need—let go of assumptions about what he or she would value. Don't assume, ask.

2. While planning your approach, ask yourself: If I get what I want, what do they get? What do they lose? Losses subtract; it's simple math. Make sure you understand any potential imbalances and address them.

3. Assess the size of the favor or agreement. If you want something big, the person on the other side will need a bigger win, too. For a great job, you need to have a very good value proposition to offer.

4. Engage your curiosity when making the request. Test your beliefs by asking questions.

5. In the case of people you know, check your 'favor bank' balance. If you're always the requestor, this can become a problem.

If this process is new to you, an example might help.

Wyatt had to organize a barbecue for his department. At first reluctant, he began to believe that he could show off his management and organizational skills. Knowing he couldn't do it alone, he sent out emails asking for help. But no one responded. Wyatt felt annoyed; he was taking on the big job of running the thing; they couldn't all just show up for fun. But when he considered telling his boss that it wasn't going to happen, he realized he didn't want a major 'fail' on his record, even if it was just a social event.

He chatted with his assigned mentor, an older woman who had worked for the company for almost 20 years. "Let me ask you something," she said. "Last time you saw an email asking for help, what did you do?"

Wyatt blinked. "I guess I thought it was spam. I ignored it."

"That's what most people do," she said. "But what if that same person came up to you and asked you to do something specific. Would that be different?" Wyatt thought about it. It would be much harder to refuse a direct response.

"And if that person had taken an extra step and thought of something that you really could do, something you excelled at, would you refuse?"

Wyatt realized that the personal touch really mattered. When people feel like they have been personally selected for a role because of their abilities, they are more likely to accept the challenge. They feel flattered. He turned around and began making a list of tasks and the people best suited for them. Wyatt was back on track.

By considering what the people you ask enjoy doing, you refocus the conversation. The request should be made in an appreciative way: You're so terrific at X; would you mind helping me? Watch out for cues that you have a mismatch. When someone demurs, this may indicate it's something they can't do or don't feel good about helping with. If you're only asking for grunt labor, make sure you're in there helping, too. No one wants to feel as if their goodwill is being taken for granted. Finally, consider what you

have done for them, and whether in a similar circumstance you would be willing to help in the same way. Are you always the requestor and not the helper? If you wouldn't drive someone to the airport, consider whether you should be asking for that kind of help.

People do enjoy feeling useful, but they have to feel good about the task as well. Otherwise, there is little in it for them. No matter what the outcome, always be very specific in your thanks. Tell them what it means to you. In a work situation, a carefully phrased email to their boss showing appreciation for their efforts is always appreciated.

A situation requiring more persuasion than a specific request would be a job interview. Many people come into this negotiation as a beggar, seeing their job as convincing a prospective employer how great they are. Some people do get jobs this way, but it isn't a reliable strategy. In a competitive market, that strategy may well leave you in second place. As mentioned in a prior chapter, one of the secrets to interviewing well is to gain an understanding of what the employer wants and needs. When you approach the interview as an equal, offering value for value, you change the dynamic.

We hire people we like, people we can envision "on the team." Your first job is to give the other person the gift of being listened to, which builds rapport and trust. Most employers also value being proven right. You have to help them see how they can be right about you. Interviewing skills were covered early, but it's helpful to be reminded that an interview is just one of the many ways WIIFM can serve you.

Though this book is focused on your career, you'll quickly see that learning how to use WIIFM effectively can be of great value in all interactions. Rather than manipulating people, what you are doing is honoring who they are and what they care about. What could be more 'win-win' than that?

Given that we all suffer from unconscious WIIFM ourselves, it's interesting that we don't anticipate it and expect it in others. Try it and see if you aren't more successful in negotiations. Win-win isn't simply a cliché; it's the successful balancing of WIIFM between parties at the deepest level.

Summary

When you understand that people unconsciously always try to act in their own best interest, you can leverage that to accomplish your work goals. Make sure when you ask for something that your request includes what the other person stands to gain by helping you. Make it much easier for people to say yes to you.

CHAPTER 21

Finding Mentors

"To be given the opportunity to help shape new artists' careers and mentor them to see their dreams come to fruition is a task I welcome with open arms."
— CHRISTINA AGUILERA, SINGER

n the early days of our country and others, people learned their trades through apprenticeships. Some trades still work that way; it can take many years to be a certified sushi chef. But for too many, you're simply expected to 'figure it out.' Management training programs, so popular in the 20th century, gave way to web training and do-it-yourself models as management cut back significantly on expenses. You're still supposed to be able to do your job, navigate the politics and become a successful employee, but with less help to make it happen.

Mentors have always been a great idea, but now you really need to consider getting one as early in your career as possible. A mentor is someone more experienced at the job, the company, or both. You're navigating two ladders to success. One involves learning how to do the job. The other is how to have the company recognize your success and help you achieve your career goals. We consult experts for a lot of things in our lives and, as one of the most important aspects, your career should receive as much attention and focus as your home repair projects, your travel plans, or any other area where you seek out advice.

A mentor can be anyone at any level of your company, even a peer who happens to have more experience than you have. In fact, many people develop a variety of mentor relationships over the course of their career. While some clients have told me that they've had difficult in find a mentor, it isn't hard, as long as you plan carefully and ask the right way. After all, most mentors will tell you that they got just as much from the relationship. It's a win-win.

Hugh found a job working in the loan department of a large bank. Thrilled to have been able to avoid the bank branch with the long hours of standing and smiling, he thought he would have it easy. Instead, he quickly found that while he could do the tasks he was given, he didn't feel he was becoming a part of the team. At noon, he'd look up and other team members had already left for lunch. He knew they had gone together when they returned as a group, laughing and relaxed.

In meetings, he would voice his opinion and then hear his words fall into a vacuum. His emails too often went unanswered. Clearly, there was a secret handshake or book of rules he was missing out on. But no one offered a hand and he struggled for months. Over time, he began to learn the way things were done at this company, but in the process fell months behind others hired after him.

While many companies have a more helpful onboarding process, not all do. And even when there is a guidebook or other information to help you, there's always more to a culture than even those in it realize. What Hugh needed was a mentor, someone who would get him started on the right foot, help him learn how things were done in this department, and set him up for success. A few forward-thinking companies assign mentors to all new hires, but most do not. So it's up to you. Only rarely does a person simply offer. You need to seek them out and ask. However, there are some guidelines that make it easier to get through this process. To prepare for the mentoring process:

1. Be clear on your objective. Where do you see yourself in one year? Five years? What do you hope the mentor will help you with?
2. Be clear on your abilities. What do you need most to succeed at your first job? To rise to the next one?
3. Select a number of people to ask, especially focusing on those who have made a similar journey to the one you want to take.
4. Define your goals for this relationship. Do you want only an interview where they share how they navigated the systems? Or do you want them to help you identify your growth areas and help you with the political challenges?
5. Understand how much time you're willing to invest. You need to be ready to take on additional activities based on what you learn from your mentor, including possibly continuing education, projects outside your normal scope, and mentoring others yourself.

6. Set up a meeting. With your goals and objectives clear in your mind, you can now ask someone to mentor you. Let them dictate frequency and time commitment.

7. Be prepared to have more than one mentor, depending on what kind of help you need and what each can offer.

Who can be your mentor? Although it is most useful in the early stages to select someone from your own company, a trusted advisor from another company can also serve in this role. Again, don't forget to consider teammates. They're the closest to remembering what you are being challenged with now. There are organizations you can consult, such as SCORE and Menttium, which offer mentoring. But it starts with you. You have to find a mentor and make the 'ask.'

As I mentioned, mentors get something out of the relationship. For some, the simple satisfaction of helping another person is enough. Most of us remember our early work days or first few months at a new company. When we didn't have help, we remember how hard it was to get started. More senior people and those about to retire are looking to fill their 'bench.' They need new people coming along to take on the next level of challenges. For ambitious people, you are rarely allowed to make the next leap in your career unless you have trained a replacement. The simple fact that you sought out help when others haven't sets you apart. It makes you look worth mentoring.

Mentors also have a potential to learn from you. As noted in the previous chapter, people from different generations see the world differently. There's nothing as rewarding as getting a new perspective on an old problem. And for many, it's inspiring to work with someone filled with ambition and energy. As you move closer to retirement, it's hard to reignite your enthusiasm-pilot. Working with younger people can do that for you. Finally, it's a great chance to get unstuck. No matter how open we think we are, all of us can find ourselves trapped in the 'that's how we've always done things' mindset. New people question.

Take that first step. Figure out what you want and start asking. While not everyone will have the time or interest, you will find mentors. As your career evolves, the early practice will serve you well. And very soon, you will have the opportunity to mentor someone else.

"I think a role model is a mentor - someone you see on a daily basis, and you learn from them."
— Denzel Washington, actor

Summary

While mentoring is of great value throughout your career, it's essential in the early stages. Make sure to go through the steps before asking someone to mentor you, so that you have a greater chance of gaining their support. Take the easier road–get a mentor.

CHAPTER 22

Email and IM Etiquette

"You never get a second chance
to make a first impression."
UNKNOWN

With people connecting around the world, emails are often the first impression your recipients have of you. With telecommuting, home offices and real offices located around the world, many of us never see our co-workers in person. The recipients of your emails often don't have a picture or any other information about you, so they make assumptions based on what they read. When your correspondent is your co-worker or remote-based manager, how you write becomes much more important. So what impressions do people have of you when they can't see you? How do they form that long-lasting impression that can come from a first contact? In most cases, it's through your emails.

More so than a hand-written note, email has an interesting problem: it's communication without the emotional content contributed by your facial expression, your voice and your body language. People can't read your expression, so they interpret your words through their own lens. Unless you're devoted to emoticons (which should be used sparingly, if at all, in a business setting), words you type peacefully could be interpreted as an attack. Emails written in haste can make people guess that you're unhappy, angry, gloating, etc. Your recipients add the tone as they interpret what you wrote. When we converse in person, we can communicate with body language and vocal variety. Face-to-face, words are one of the least important factors in how people process the information. In email, words are all you have. What you write must say what you mean.

In the modern workplace, email has replaced many other forms of communication.[3] Many write an email before they even consider picking up a phone. How careful are you with those many quick missives? Many people have inadvertently blocked career advancement and new opportunities with their poorly constructed emails. Even when the results aren't quite as serious, poor email communications can make people think less of you or more easily misunderstand you. Could this be true of you?

Marshawn came straight from college into a career position at a building management company. Most of his colleagues were older people, so he knew they weren't comfortable with his favorite method of communication, texting. He quickly learned that most communication was through email, all

---

3 Though texting is quite popular as well, it is rare to text people in the workplace unless you already know them.

of which was archived in case it was needed in some legal matter.

In early one-on-ones with his manager, Marshawn had been warned: his emails were very informal and not grammatically correct. He used a lot of slang, and his manager suggested that his style was too casual for the culture he was in. She suggested that he work on improving them. In fact, she told him he would have to or it could be a serious problem.

Marshawn was confused. What more could he do? He reviewed his emails and they sounded just the way he spoke. No one criticized that. What could he do better?

Here are some points to consider when you hit the keyboard, especially when the communication is important or will be sent to people you don't know well. These casual "notes" are letters and should be treated as such. They can and will be saved or printed, and can be used against you. Deleting emails won't help you. In most cases, they're stored on a server, and in some cases they may end up in your personnel file.

Remember what emails are for: they are to communicate. At work, you are often talking about some work that needs to be done. These emails must indicate clearly what work is expected, when it is due, and what the result should look like.

For really important emails, it can be useful to draft them in a Word document and edit them there. You can always copy and paste them when they are ready. It helps to avoid the dreaded 'auto-send' situation. When you shine at email, you stand out at work in a good way. Writing is a rapidly vanishing skill, but an increasingly important one. This can be a career-differentiator.

Basic Guidelines

1. **Spelling.** Get it right. Do not rely on spell check–it can't distinguish between your and you're or their/they're/there. Missed letters in a word may still result in a viable word, just not the one you meant to type. Auto-correct can change well-crafted thoughts into something embarrassing. Particularly when your field relies on industry-specific jargon or acronyms, mistakes can be at best confusing and at worst career-limiting.

2. **Grammar.** Learn some basic rules. Terrible grammar may not be detected as such, but when you use words such as 'ain't,' you leave an impression that you aren't educated. For a quick and valuable read, consult Strunk and White, **"The Elements of Style."** Some things never go out of style. Word will help with this, but most email programs will not.

3. **Avoid IMisms.** Not everyone texts, and using text shorthand can make your message hard to read. Only use abbreviations and acronyms that are in common use in your industry. There are only so many three-letter acronyms possible, and the reality is that there are multiple meanings for each one. Check out http://www.acronymfinder.com/ and prepare to be amazed. Also, for grins, google 'old people text abbreviations.' Many stories rebound with such misunderstandings as one mother's LOL meaning 'lots of love' instead of 'laughing out loud.'

4. **Avoid slang and cultural references.** Emails get forwarded, and outside the United States, or even

between regions, slang and cultural references, including idioms, may be misunderstood. Reread your email as if you're speaking English as a second language; consider that words are more likely to be interpreted literally. A boot is a car trunk in England, and yet giving someone the boot in America means to fire them. In some cases, these misunderstandings can become the basis for a sexual harassment suit. An administrative assistant was horrified to be asked for a rubber by a new colleague from the UK. All he really wanted was an eraser. He also noted that she looked "all knocked up," which in his idiom meant that she looked tired. You can see how this could become an HR issue.

5. **Use complete sentences.** This is a reflection of your ability to communicate clearly.

6. **Make your point clearly.** This means using nouns that communicate. Always reread an email before you send it. Would you understand it if you received it hours later? Is the context clear?

7. **Who, what, when, why and how.** When you make a request, test it for the 4-W's, and sometimes the 'How.' A clear request saves time, eliminates endless emails back and forth, and also avoids disappointment with the result. This helps the person you are asking so he is able to deliver quickly on your request.

8. **Use humor with care.** Where a spoken anecdote might work well, without your facial expression, body language and intonation, humor may fall flat or just offend.

9. **Avoid group spam.** Use SEND ALL or RESPOND ALL with great care. Consider never using it, so that you have to consciously decide who should receive your missive.

10. **Remember "please" and "thank you".** Use these terms generously in emails. In the United States, it can add a personal note to use the person's first name to address them as you begin the body of the email. When addressing anyone from a different country, make sure you know their cultural preferences.

11. **Type your key point or call to action in the subject line.** The clearer you make the subject line, the easier it is for someone to remember your request and to find it later. If people have told you that your emails often end up in their spam folder, you now know why. When you use the subject line in a smart way, you're likely to get faster responses.

12. **Tailor email style to your recipient.** Use formal styles for emails to superiors, be formal, yet engaging to customers.

13. **Use 'urgent' or similar words sparingly.** In a work situation, urgent means 'drop everything and do this.' Use it only when really necessary.

14. **Don't assume—write it down.** Even if you have just finished a telephone call with someone, write down and share your understanding. The email should stand on its own, without the recipient having to remember the call or link it to other emails. It also gives you a communication trail, a valuable asset in a work world rife with multi-tasking and over-commitments.

Less Obvious Rules

1. **The law.** At work, consider the legal implications of an email. Don't say it in writing if it might be used against you or your company. Use the following tests: Would you be okay if your email showed up in tomorrow's paper? If someone still had your email five years from now, would that be an issue?

2. **Judgment.** Praise in email, criticize by phone or in person. Use the same rule with good or bad news.

3. **Emotion.** Express emotion by telephone or in person, unless you can be very clear. Just as with humor, strong emotion reads differently in text. Even when you have no intention of sounding angry or unhappy, a poor choice of words can communicate emotion when none is meant. When you can, read your email out loud. Check that it sounds the way you want it to sound and that you have chosen the best words to convey your meaning.

4. **Absolutes.** Be cautious with the use of the words 'all,' 'none,' always' or 'never.' As with verbal communications, absolutes do not leave room for negotiation. For some recipients, the use of these words can set them off, when you had no intention of being controversial.

5. **Signatures.** Craft a professional signature line with email and phone information, company name, etc. It can be helpful to include information regarding time zone for those multi-national companies. This helps set expectations regarding availability.

6. **Pick up the phone.** When the email thread gets long enough and you can't follow where it's going, call your correspondent. Technology isn't always our friend.

7. **Protect Yourself.** It can be useful to save a copy of an email so that you have proof of its content and the date and time you sent it. Just don't make it a default. With the volume of emails these days, the amount of storage you have been allocated can quickly be filled with all the emails you save. If it's important, print out the email and save it in your personal files.

8. **Recheck the Email Address:** Misaddressed emails can be fatal. Imagine sending confidential information to the wrong person! With most email programs designed to help you "complete the address," it can be easy to send your email to someone else.

9. **Know which emails to save.** Your company may have a policy of saving all emails on a server, but it can be hard to find the ones you need in that collection. Make a folder for your kudos, the compliments and praise you get. Consider saving other important emails in a folder for a period of time. Especially over the course of a project, you may be surprised how happy you are to find that you can refer back to these emails.

Exercise 22-1: With these guidelines in mind, review a few recent emails. Read them as if you were the recipient. Did you accomplish what you wanted to with your words? Could any of it lead to a less favorable impression of you? Make note of the areas where you have problems so you can be alert to them in the future.

QUICK TIP: Even when simply emailing a friend from your work PC, be cautious. Injudicious emails can be accidently forwarded and may end up in your Human Resources file. Use your personal email accounts for personal emails. If in doubt, use the phone.

Another aspect of email etiquette that is important is how and when you check your email. Though you can see people everywhere bent over a phone, constantly checking mail, texting and searching, in the workplace, the rules are a little different.

Briana had been hooked on her iPhone since the first day she got it as a graduation gift. So much easier to use than her father's hand-me-down Blackberry, she couldn't resist checking it constantly and keeping her friends up-to-date on Instagram and other sites. Her job as a customer support engineer at a search engine company kept her focused on answering customer questions most of the workday, so when she had a chance to pull her phone out, she took it, even if it was during one of the staff meetings or training sessions. A few others did the same, at times. Briana tried to limit it, but when she felt the vibration, she couldn't resist the temptation to check.

One day, during an all-hands meeting, she suddenly realized that the room had gone quiet. The CIO stood quietly at the lectern and everyone was looking at her. Had she missed something? A colleague pointed to her phone and shook his head. Briana realized she had missed an announcement requiring all devices be turned off. She turned her phone off and the meeting resumed, but she wondered how much it would hurt her that she had disrespected the CIO.

You will see C-level managers make this mistake, but earlier in your career, being too tightly 'leashed' to your device can cost you. Remember that one of the greatest gifts you can give someone is your undivided attention. Even if you are the only one with your device tucked away, imagine how the speaker will feel. He will remember you.

Most of this chapter deals with general emails, but emails to clients and senior managers at your own company require a bit more from you. This is when you want to show off your best. Clarity and professionalism are even more important. Colleagues will generally tolerate a more casual approach. Clients and your management team may judge you on your email competence. For a special situation—a big request, a big thank you, or other important items—consider opening up Word (or another word processing program) and writing a real letter. Then print it and put it in the mail. Not only will practice in the fine art of letter writing improve your emails, it sets you apart from others and underlines your professionalism. And most people enjoy getting a personal letter; we all get too much impersonal mail.

Most companies now include an instant message capability on corporate systems. This can be a huge time-saver, but it can also be a career-limiter. A quick IM can net you a fast answer, letting you get your work done without a major interruption of someone else's work. But how often do we find ourselves caught up in a number of IM sessions?

Teresa got bored during the annual corporate meeting. Streamed live from headquarters, most employees were watching it online from their cubicles or home offices. New to her job, she really didn't understand the financials and wondered why she needed to know that level of detail. Idly, she began to IM with a colleague in the next room. Another window popped up and she began responding to that one. Clearly, everyone was bored. In a few minutes, she had 10 windows open and was trying to keep up with the chatter. She didn't notice that one window was her manager asking her if she understood the implication of a loss that had just been mentioned. Teresa realized to her horror that she had responded to her manager with an answer to someone else's question, an inappropriate response at best and possibly offensive at worst.

It's hard to stay on top of all those windows, so consider putting yourself offline when you need to focus. Another aspect is the fact that, while seeming small, all IMs are interruptions. Use them carefully to elicit a quick answer. If you need more information, use IM to ask for a quick call. Or simply set up a meeting. When used appropriately, IM is a powerful tool, but it can be abused.

When people talk about the importance of soft skills in the market, communication is the most requested. Emails and IMs are a major portion of communication today; you can't afford not to get it right.

"With me it's always about first impressions."
Billy Zane, actor

Summary

Emails and instant messages offer many ways to derail your career. By focusing on the suggestions in this chapter, you can ensure that your messages reflect your brand and help you to stand out. Both types of communications are stored on servers, so managers can go back and see problem patterns. Give them only great work and it sends a strong, subtle message of your professionalism.

CHAPTER 23

Friendships at Work

We have a natural urge to connect with people we meet and then develop relationships. This is how we made friends as children, and later created lasting connections at college. But work is different. While some of us throw ourselves into friendships easily and others are slower to bond, connections at work should be managed more carefully. Move slowly to welcome people into your inner circle of friendship. Enjoy relationships at work, but take time before connecting with your colleagues outside of work.

Stephanie loved people. "The more friends, the merrier," she always said. When she began her first job, she made friends easily and after a few times going out to lunch with several of them, began inviting them to parties. One of her favorites, Kyle, was slightly older than the rest and had been on the job longer than most of them. She indicated her strong interest in him, and was disappointed at the cool reception she received.

A few months after she started, the company had a major reorg and Kyle was promoted to manage her group. Stephanie felt he treated her more harshly than others in the group and this broke the small bond she felt they had together. When she could she resolved to try to change groups, but at her company, you had to stay in a position for a year. She knew it would be a long year.

It's impossible not to like some people more than others at work. And over time, it's likely you will discover people with whom you want to have a deeper friendship. But the most important aspect of working together is preserving the respect and, yes, the distance needed to be able to team with anyone and get the job done. Especially if you are new to an area, having moved to take the job you now have, it can be tempting to use work as a source for your new friendships. But take the time to develop them slowly and look elsewhere for immediate connections.

Friends often share intimate details of their lives, and you want to be sure not only that you can trust that person, but that no one at work has information you don't want shared with others. It's very easy for subjects to come up in conversation. For many, gossip is just too much fun. Work is different. Like a sports team, it requires us to work with every other person on a project, whether we like them or not. To make that work, you want to build relationships slowly, focusing first on simply getting the job done.

This means that you need to avoid getting emotionally involved with someone at work. While it can happen, there are many cases where one or the other member of a couple had to move to a new department or leave the company because the relationship interfered with work. Remember that professors weren't allowed to date students. There's a good reason for it. Work is much the same.

But this doesn't mean being aloof either. If you're a little shy, it can be easy to eat lunch at your desk. Instead, invite someone you work with to lunch. Lunch is where people begin to connect and people we like are simply easier to work with. Even if someone seems like they aren't your kind of person, give it a try. You may find a great connection.

> Joel didn't feel he had anything in common with Carlos. Carlos grew up in the Central Valley of California in a small town; he came from Manhattan. He had gone to a prep school, then a prestigious college; Carlos had only gone to junior college and had his AA. Encouraged by a friend to reach out a little more, Joel invited Carlos to lunch. As they began to talk, they discovered a shared passion for baseball, even though they disagreed on which team was best. Joel also learned that Carlos enjoyed hiking, especially on vacation. With that, they had many subjects to discuss and he felt more comfortable working with Carlos after that lunch.

People at work may be the main people you meet, but by remembering to take it slowly, you will find that you won't end up in an uncomfortable situation, nor will you damage your career.

Summary

Work friendships can be a landmine unless you remember to take it slowly. Try to find connections of some kind with every colleague and avoid, where possible, romantic encounters. You have the opportunity to create lifetime friendships that enhance rather than hurt your career.

CHAPTER 24

Working Remotely and Succeeding

"I'm always working. I work wherever I am."
L'WREN SCOTT, FASHION DESIGNER

Today, some positions are either work from home or working from a satellite office remote from the rest of your team. For many, this presents a huge benefit. You can save on time and money—no commuting can really transform your life. You save on clothes. While it's a good idea to be dressed, jeans and tees or other casual attire is perfectly acceptable. In a global economy, it's a lot easier getting going for a 6AM call when you merely have to roll out of bed to take it. Still, there are tradeoffs.

The acronym for the famous computer hardware and software manufacturer, IBM, once meant "I've Been Moved." Now it means "I'm By Myself." Some people function better in an office environment and enjoy the camaraderie of the direct connection.

When your technology fails you at home, while there may be online support, you're mostly on your own. Despite the significant savings to the company of not having to rent office space, equipment and furniture, most are fairly cheap on providing you with money to buy your own. Need a toner cartridge, paper or more pens? Head out to your office supply store and buy some. In general, though, you save more than you spend, and time is worth a lot.

Managed well, this can be a win-win. Bosses will notice those self-disciplined and determined folks who manage their workload and priorities with ease. Managed poorly, this work arrangement can negatively impact both your career and your personal life. Working remotely does change things. It can be easier in some ways than telecommuting, where you have an office at home and one at your workplace. Your work tools and materials are at hand. You don't have to figure out what to bring back and forth. You're at home, so you don't need to align in-person meetings with your commute schedule.

The downside is that you may find it "out of sight, out of mind." Many managers are still stuck in the past and believe in "managing by walking around." They find it far more challenging to manage a team that isn't in view. If your entire team is remote, it can help quite a bit because you're all sharing the same challenges. Still, it isn't the same as working in the same building as your manager.

You have to work differently to ensure your "presence" is valued and recognized.

Reniqa began her career with a cubical in a nice office. She thrived in the office environment, where interaction with colleagues kept her ideas flowing and her energy high. Her parents' careers had led her to expect an office environment, and she enjoyed dressing for work and having lunch with co-workers.

After a merger, the company decided to save money by eliminating property. Her office was the first to close. Her entire team was sent to work from home. Reniqa doubted this would work for her. She shared her tiny apartment with a friend, but there was no extra space for a home office. She had to buy furniture and cram her supplies and files into a small space. One big challenge was finding the discipline to work in an environment where there were so many attractive alternatives.

But the worst part was communication. After being able to simply 'drop in' on someone, she found that she had to try to reach distant colleagues by phone or email. People seemed too casual about email requests; she found she had to ping people over and over to get a response. Her new manager lived 2,000 miles away, so she had a time zone issue to contend with.

After a smooth start in the office, Reniqa became concerned about her future. How could she show up and differentiate herself while working remotely? What did she need to do to make sure she wasn't forgotten?

Here are some guidelines to keep you as "connected" as you ever were in an office, while ensuring you still have a life.

1. **Communicate** – In an office, you're visible, even if head-down while working on a project. At home, you're invisible. Keep yourself front and center by:

- **Using the phone**. Don't email or IM all the time: call. You need the immediacy. If an IM session goes on for a while, pick up the phone.
- **Setting up phone meetings**. Do this even if it's only to bounce ideas off others. All will benefit. It helps to replace the hallway discussions that used to ignite productive creativity.
- **Scheduling regular meetings with your manager.** Prepare an agenda and connect with him or her.
- **Keeping (and sharing) status reports.** No one can "see" what you do anymore, so you need to tell them. Don't be modest or shy.
- **Making all communications professional.** They're your "face" in the office
- **Responding promptly to calls and emails.** Even if you can't complete the requested task immediately, let someone know. Show up as if you're there, even when you're not.

QUICK TIP: Unless your company forbids it, invest in Skype or Vonage. Use your IP phone so you don't have an excuse that the calls will cost you too much. Exploit your company conferencing service. Use Facetime or another free cell phone calling feature. And make sure you have a headset. Be comfortable on the phone and you will do it more frequently.

2. **Team.** Even when alone, you're part of a larger organization. Take advantage of it. All projects are improved by multiple perspectives. Seek out ways to work with others.

3. **Build relationships**. Seek out people to connect with and share information. Who else does the same kind of work that you do? What can you learn from them? What can you offer? Schedule virtual lunches and virtual coffee breaks with colleagues. Send relevant articles and links you find to others. Share what you know.

4. **Be incredibly responsible.** Make only work commitments you can keep, and then produce work that you can take pride in. Remember to under-promise and over-deliver. Work time is work time–get the stuff done. Home distractions are numerous, and yet you need to find a way to ignore them. You aren't "at home" when you're working.

5. **Create a good work environment**. Even if the space you carve out at home is small, make it work for you. Have the tools, machines and supplies you need near to hand. Invest in a multi-machine: printer, copier and scanner. Have a sturdy file cabinet. Keep home and non-work items out of this space, and keep the space organized. In some cases, you can take a tax deduction for this space, but make sure to talk with a tax accountant to understand the rules.

6. **Be ready to work**. Shower and get dressed each morning. You don't need to put on the same kinds of clothes you'd choose to wear in an office, but make sure what you choose makes you feel professional and "at work." You'll take yourself and your work more seriously. The way you look and feel shows up on the phone. They may not know why, but callers can tell.

7. **Define a work day.** When at work, be at work. Communicate your hours and be there when you say you will. You can have a flexible schedule as long as

everyone knows what it is. By defining it, you help to ensure that your work day isn't your whole day.

8. **Invest in a web-cam.** When you can "see" someone, they're more present than when they're simply a voice on the phone. Use the web-cam with Skype or other IP phone capability to emulate an "in-person experience."

If you behave like the professional you are, you will be seen that way. Doing this validates the company's trust in you and ensures your status as a valued contributor.

Justin really liked the concept of working from home. Although he loved riding his motorcycle on the weekends, being bogged down in commute traffic for hours was a nightmare to him. Quickly, he realized that he had to work differently. Used to having someone watching over his work all the time, he knew he had to make some changes. So he talked to his parents, both of whom had worked from home at various times.

Using their tips, he began by volunteering his status report each week and scheduling regular meetings with his boss. Despite his personal desire to text everyone when he had a question or comment, he started using the phone more often and was surprised how productive it was. Texting dialogues that might last a half hour could be accomplished in minutes on the phone.

He developed a ritual matching the way he thought he would be at work, giving himself a clear start and end time, breaks and a defined, yet short, lunch period. On the rare occasions where he had to go into the office, he dressed for success and made sure to plan a lunch date so he could reconnect with teammates. After a few months, though he missed the camaraderie of co-workers, he found that he could be effective and happy on the job.

These tips will help you succeed while working from home. But being home-officed has the potential to cause problems to work-life balance. Consider these items to ensure that work doesn't overshadow your life.

1. **Leave work**. Work your hours and then leave work behind. Develop an 'end of day' ritual. Except in emergencies, treat nights and weekends the same way you did when you went into an office. You have the right to your time off and, more importantly, you need it. You won't be at your best working 80-hour weeks.

2. **Watch out for technical distractions**. Smartphones make it possible to stay constantly connected to work into the early hours of the morning, on weekends and even on your vacation. When you're not at work, turn the device off or leave it somewhere. Prioritize and only respond to what you must. Do not be leashed to devices. It's also useful to limit checking email while trying to get a task accomplished. Frequent distractions don't lead to quality work. Studies prove that multi-tasking doesn't really work. Every time you switch your focus, you have to move your concentration. This takes time and also distracts your brain. Be conscious of the temptation to constantly 'check in.'

3. **Eat breakfast and lunch, and take breaks**. Come back refreshed and energized. It's too easy to skip these or

shortchange them, but you shortchange yourself as well as your work. In the long run, you will sacrifice your health if you do not take care of yourself.

4. **Family and friends should be well up in your priorities**. Define time for them and for your hobbies, and then take it. Guard this time. You aren't serving anyone by putting work first all the time. If you don't get this right, you might find you have nothing else.

5. **Change clothes after work**. Go out to your health club. Put on tennis shoes and take a walk.

6. **Take your real sick days**. Since you technically can force yourself into your office chair and answer email, it's easy to never consider yourself "too sick to work." You will be sick longer and recover slower if you don't care for yourself first.

7. **Take real vacations.** Delegate your work and leave it behind. If you don't ensure that you get real time off, no one else will be there to ensure you do.

QUICK TIP: Take a short walk at lunch. Most office workers get out more than home workers, and the benefit of fresh air and sunshine is substantial. Recent studies have proven that difficult problems and challenges magically disappear when you get out and walk, even when you don't spend a second consciously thinking about those issues. There's something about the combination of nature and movement that helps your brain get past any roadblocks.

Summary

Working from home can be a blessing, but it can also be a challenge. When you make a strong effort to be 'present' to your manager with quality work, regular updates and regular meetings, you can avoid being forgotten. But, at the same time, working from home can lead to being 'always on.' Make sure you take the time off you're entitled to and give your phone a rest.

CHAPTER 25

How to Ask for Money or a Promotion

> "Don't lower your expectations to meet your performance. Raise your level of performance to meet your expectations. Expect the best of yourself, and then do what is necessary to make it a reality."
> Ralph Marston, 'The Daily Motivator'

n the after-school or summer job world, raises and promotions come along rarely and, in most cases, you don't ask for them. In a career job, while some raises may simply depend on performance, it helps to understand how the process works, so you have an idea how you can influence the process.

At each job level, there will be a salary band, a range of pay that is considered appropriate for that title. You probably won't know what that is, but when companies bring a new hire in, they tend to try to offer a salary at the lower end of that band. Where you are in the band can affect how much more they will pay you. The dollar amount also matters. If you make a six-figure salary, a 3% raise is a lot more money than if you make only $20,000. If you are at top of a band, you may not be eligible for a raise until you get a promotion.

When a company starts planning for raises, a set amount of money is put aside for raises. The managers rank their teams on performance and, based on the rankings and factors--such as where you are in the band or how essential you are to team deliverables--they assign a raise amount to you. By the time they begin planning, it's too late, in most cases, to negotiate. At this point, anything more they give to you means less they can offer others.

However, when you make a compelling argument earlier, a manager can make a case that his team (or you) warrants additional money. So the goal is to make your case at the right time and to present a very strong argument.

Harry had been very anxious to land a job quickly as his college debts were scaring him. After six months, he realized that he had probably settled for too little money and really deserved more. He had checked salary surveys and job sites; he had the evidence he felt he needed to argue for a raise. Besides, he had been doing a great job since he started. He approached his manager, Geneva.

"Geneva," he said, "I'd like to ask for a raise based on my performance this past year."

Geneva frowned. "Did you realize it was review time?" She handed him his draft review. To his shock, she had rated him as 'average' or 'meets.'

"Geneva," he said, "You know how much I've done for the company so far. And these surveys indicate that I came in under the normal pay for this job."

Geneva shook her head. "You accepted the offer. And this year, those who only get a 'meets' aren't getting a raise. There's just not much money to give out."

Harry couldn't believe it. When he suggested that he needed help because his student loans took such a huge part of his paycheck, Geneva said, "Maybe you should have managed your money better."

As companies lay people off or force them into early retirement, you may have found that you are expected to take on more work, but you aren't compensated for it. Most of us need more money each year, not less. If you are working the "hope for change" method as Harry did, you will probably not be successful. "Hope for change" means hoping management will grant you a large raise during the annual review period without being asked.

When you do this, you are making the assumption that the manager can't wait to reward your good work, and also has the discretion to reward individuals monetarily. I like to draw on a favorite coaching question, "How's that working for you?" Even in a good job market, people who rely on the "hope for change" model only received more when there was a threat (implied or real) that the employee was ready to leave for more money. Though it may have appeared that this method worked in some cases, ultimatums rarely leave either side feeling that a win/win has been achieved. This technique can backfire. If your manager doesn't believe that you deserve the raise, you may find yourself on the target layoff list. At the very least, he will expect you to prove your value after the fact.

If he recognizes that you are really unhappy about the situation, he may assume that you will use work time to find a better job, if you don't leave when you threaten. Ultimatums only work if you're ready to leave and have a great offer. Only in some cases will your current company be willing to go even further than the new one to keep you. You may see these actions as prudent career management; managers often see this as disloyalty.

So what works? As Harry did, some people believe in simply asking for a raise at review time. This seems to make sense, because that is often when money has been allocated for this purpose. For those employing the direct approach, the problem is the timing. As noted above, the money has already been decided at that point. Another problem is that quite a few people phrase their request in terms of why they need the raise. Personal expenses, comparison to salaries of other people and the length of time since the last raise, are all approaches that have been tried and failed. "But I really need more money," you might say. The answer is harsh, but true: your boss DOES NOT CARE. While he or she might like you personally and, in that light, sympathize with your plight, it will make no difference. Companies are in business to make money. Thus, they don't care that:

- You have a new child.
- You have huge college loans to pay.
- You now have elderly parents to support.
- Your bills have gotten out of control.
- You realize belatedly that you need to be saving more for retirement.

As people, managers care.   But as managers, they can't base their decisions on your personal needs.   In addition, how they manage their budgets is part of how they are rated. If a manager is deemed unable to manage their expenses, this will raise a lot of red flags. Defining your salary request as a 'need for money' is a negative, no matter whether your manager fears that your financial woes will lead to less diligent work or if they feel some concern that you might be tempted to steal from the company or even embezzle, if in such a position.

Since leading with your needs is not a recipe for success, what works? Giving you a raise (keeping you happy) must be in the interest of your employer. In most cases, your manager will have to argue your case to higher levels, so he must believe that you have established a good case.

To build your case:

1. Ask for a raise after a particularly great performance review or the completion of a major project. When you can demonstrate success, you are more likely to prevail. The latter is an especially good time, as money may have already been allocated by the time your review is done.

2. Quantify your value to the company. If you have saved or made them money, document the facts. Though some major accomplishments may not have any impact on revenue for the company, any way you can tie your results to money will more easily translate to salary increases to you.

3. Document your differentiators. How do you compare to others at your level? It isn't about what others make, but about what you do relative to your peers and how it contributes to corporate success. How innovative are

you? How does your communication (writing/speaking) and teamwork compare to others? How much faster are you at getting things done?

4. If you know that you're below market value, bring documentation of this. If not, don't despair. This is only one facet of your case and it can't be the only facet. Too many factors go into these surveys, including years of experience, certifications, cost of living in the area, and the unemployment factor. Higher rates of unemployment (more demand for jobs) will translate to lower salaries for those who can get a job.

5. Document your value to the business: institutional knowledge is invaluable whereas training a new hire takes time. At the same time, be prepared to demonstrate that knowledge and explain how you have gone the extra mile, e.g., mentored someone, created training, or automated some procedure.

6. Collect letters of praise and recognition for these meetings.

7. Determine what you will accept in a raise. In most cases, raises are finite–you might want a 50% raise, but you're unlikely to get it. If little money is available now, ask them to reconsider your request in six months, rather than waiting for the next raise cycle.

8. Finally, schedule time with your manager. Treat this as a business proposal. If you don't have a case after reviewing this list, then perhaps you need to wait until you're better prepared before presenting it. If you're refused, ask what you can do to earn a raise six months from now. Get concrete objectives.

QUICK TIP: Don't threaten unless you have plans to go anyway. Keep the discussion positive and focused on your value. Stress that you'd love to stay, but you have to make choices based on what is right for your family and what best reflects your value. All of this is much easier if you have skillfully highlighted your accomplishments all along, both to your manager and to those above that level.

Everyone wants to be a good person and be able to reward their people. You have to understand that they can't do this for everyone. Make sure you're on the radar with them, so your name comes forward.

How can you stand out? Don't wait for your review. If your manager is interested, provide a weekly status report, pitching your accomplishments in terms of how they benefit the company. If not, still keep a running list of accomplishments that you periodically share with your manager. Review the list with him or her on a regular basis, making sure to tie your work efforts to corporate goals, if possible. Check in with others to understand financial implications. Real numbers have more of an impact than anything else. These same kinds of numbers are also useful for a résumé.

Devony had a good list when she asked Sue for a raise: "In the past quarter, I closed 15% more customer issues than the team goals. For every emergency issue I was assigned, I resolved the problem in half the time expected, leading to five customer 'thank you' letters. Our sales team has told me that, because of the service improvements, they've been able to close deals in half the time and, in most cases, sell at least 25% more product.

"For example, Bernie just told me about a deal with SY Company. He had expected it to take a year to close, but when he showed our support numbers, they signed much more quickly."

With concrete results like this, it made it easier for Sue to argue Devony's case. Remember that Devony never mentioned that she needed the money. She only focused on why she deserved it.

Still, in many cases, there simply isn't money available at the time to reward great performance. There are other options open to managers that you could consider. Consider asking if a bonus or profit-sharing might be possible. The point is to show that you know your business, made a major contribution and understand and are committed to company goals.

Other options are to ask for some extra time off, additional education, upgraded equipment, and more. Some of these benefits are tax write-offs for the company, which is desirable for your employer. Non-salary benefits often don't increase your taxable income, a desirable outcome. Even if they can't do anything for you now, make sure that your accomplishments are well-documented in your file. This gives weight to the argument that you deserve more when money becomes available.

Believe in yourself and your value, so you can sell it. While we generally know our weaknesses and can get focused on them, this is the time to recognize achievement and accomplishment.

"Be a yardstick of quality. Some people aren't used to an environment where excellence is expected."
Steve Jobs, CEO, innovator

Summary

To get a raise or a promotion, you have to prove you have earned it. Pitch your case in terms of delivering on company goals. The more you tie your success to the things your company cares about, the easier it is to recognize your value in dollars.

END NOTES

"Your work is going to fill a large part of your life, and the only way to be truly satisfied is to do what you believe is great work. And the only way to do great work is to love what you do. If you haven't found it yet, keep looking. Don't settle. As with all matters of the heart, you'll know when you find it."
Steve Jobs, CEO

You are taking the first step into your adult future by beginning your career. Whether times are tough and jobs are scarce, there will always be a position for the best prepared; the one who understands what it takes to succeed. **First Job Savvy** was designed to help you maximize your opportunities and stand out in a crowded field of applicants.

While it may seem intimidating, take one step at a time and realize that your uniqueness, your talent, and your latent abilities will be recognized and rewarded when you find the way to shout them out so hiring managers can hear them. In our work lives, many of us will have a wide variety of jobs and careers. The goal now is just to get started on it, to get away from the minimum wage, perhaps mindless work you had to do to get through school.

You may not believe it right now, but this journey will be fun as well as hard work. We're at our best when we're not exactly sure we can accomplish something; where we stand on the edge of a cliff and jump. There's no drug like the adrenaline rush of challenging your assumptions, going past where you think you can go and making it happen. Take the first step today.

"People should pursue what they're passionate about. That will make them happier than pretty much anything else."
— Elon Musk, CEO & inventor

Resources

The resources listed here were current at time of publication. As sites come and go, some of these may no longer be relevant or available. The title of each section offers keywords you can use to do your own search. This may also be a good option if the sites I have suggested don't work for you.

Ch 1 – Assess Yourself
Value Inventories:
http://www.lifevaluesinventory.org/

Ch 3 – Resources for matching a job to your 'Happiness Intersection'
Skills profilers or assessments:
http://careerplanning.about.com/od/selfassessment/
http://assessment.com/
http://www.careerinfonet.org/skills/default.aspx?nodeid=20

http://www.onetonline.org/skills/
http://www.iseek.org/careers/skillsAssessment
http://www.careeronestop.org/ExploreCareers/SelfAssessments/
FindAssessments.aspx
Occupational Outlook Handbook
http://www.bls.gov/ooh/
Career lists:
http://www.career-descriptions-and-jobs.com/list-of-career.html
http://www.careerplanner.com/ListOfCareers.cfm
http://www.careerprofiles.info/careers.html

Ch 4 – Résumé Help

Sample résumé and templates: http://jobsearch.about.com/od/
resumes/
Résumé do's and don'ts: http://www.quintcareers.com/resume-dos-
donts.html
Books:
**Resume Magic, 4th Ed: Trade Secrets of a Professional Resume
Writer (Resume Magic: Trade Secrets of a Professional Resume
Writer) -** Susan Britton Whitcomb
**Resume Writing 2015: Up-to-date Resume Writing Guide to
Get You Hired in 2015 –** Ashley Tucker

Ch 5 – Managing Your
Social Presence

Useful information:
http://www.forbes.com/sites/susanadams/2013/03/14/6-
steps-to-managing-your-online-reputation/

http://www.forbes.com/sites/johnrampton/2014/09/29/25-ways-to-grow-your-social-media-presence/

Ch 6 – Networks
http://www.inc.com/patricia-fletcher/what-are-6-ways-you-can-create-a-strong-network.html
http://shepalearning.com/personal-networks-steps/
http://www.meetup.com – find common interests here

Ch 7 – Research Companies
http://jobsearch.about.com/od/interviews/qt/interviewtipcompany.htm
http://jobsearch.about.com/od/companyresearch/a/badcompany.htm
http://jobsearch.about.com/od/companyresearch/a/jobresearch.htm

Ch 8 – Understanding your intrinsic self as a way to match with a company
Conation – your intrinsic strengths:
http://kolbe.com/why-kolbe/
Assessment tool:
http://kolbe.com/assessments/kolbe-a-index/ $49.95 for a comprehensive insight

Ch 9 – LinkedIn Help

In your search engine, type in "LinkedIn video tutorials." You'll find many dealing with all aspects of using LinkedIn, from setting up your profile to managing it to finding jobs through it.

Ch 12 – How to Conduct Informational Interviews

http://jobsearch.about.com/cs/infointerviews/a/infointerview.htm

http://www.quintcareers.com/informational_interviewing.html

http://www.quintcareers.com/information_interview.html

http://www.forbes.com/sites/susanadams/2015/03/04/30-questions-to-ask-in-an-informational-interview/

Ch 13 – Interview Preparation

https://www.readyprepinterview.com/

http://career-advice.monster.com/job-interview/careers.aspx

http://career-advice.monster.com/job-interview/interview-preparation/what-if-your-interview-is-tomorrow/article.aspx

http://jobsearch.about.com/od/interviewquestionsanswers/a/interviewquest.htm

Ch 15 – Making the Deal

Salary range sites:

http://www1.salary.com/Salary-Ranges.html

http://www.salary.com/

http://www.payscale.com/

http://coach.careerbuilder.com/

Ch 16 – Paperwork

Legal issues in the workplace:
http://www.nolo.com/legal-encyclopedia/hr-employment-law
http://www.workplacefairness.org/

Ch 21 – Mentoring

http://www.quintcareers.com/mentor_value.html
http://www.forbes.com/sites/susanadams/2014/03/14/
how-to-find-and-use-a-mentor-3/
http://dgsomdiversity.ucla.edu/workfiles/lectures/Making%20
the%20Most%20of%20Mentors.pdf

Acknowledgements

Writing itself is a solitary craft, but no writer gets through it alone. As I finish writing this book, I wish to recognize all the people who helped me realize my dream for this book. My husband, Mike, patiently encouraged me, read my many drafts and kept me sane when I wondered if I could finish it. He had great suggestions, all of which are included here. While I had to do the writing, a book is immeasurably improved when you get additional perspectives on the subject.

Next, I want to thank the Pleasant Hill Writer's Group, Write On; my critique group friends. The core group--Alicia Watson, Heidi Young and Nancy Hume--provided much-needed advice and counsel. Every writer needs people who will tell the truth. Without this, no book would be as good.

My reviewers include: Felicia Harris, Merideth Mehlberg, Laura Donovan and Mary Thomas. I am very grateful that they were willing to take the time and say something about my book.

John and Dane Low provided the e-book formatting and cover art.

And finally, I thank my coaching clients who inspired this book and helped me learn a great deal about what works and what doesn't. Their successes helped me realize that my individual coaching doesn't scale. I wrote the book for all those I can't coach personally.

Note to Readers

Dear Readers,

Thank you for buying/reading this book. Although I love to create fiction, I found myself drawn to writing career books instead because I saw my friends and their children struggling to keep and find jobs. Over the years, in my own career and as I coached others, I learned a lot about what works and what doesn't. I knew I had to share this information. There are no guarantees in life, but these techniques will allow you to seize control of your career, instead of drifting like a leaf caught in the tide.

As a writer, I am excited to share what I know, but I also want to learn what you liked about it and how the information contributed to your career success. And I also want to know when I get it wrong or when I missed some areas that you feel were important. Please talk to me at denise@dpkcoaching.com or my Twitter handle

@denisekalm. People who follow me will get updates when I learn more.

A challenge in these days of too-easy publishing is to get the word out to readers. You'd be doing me a great favor if you'd mention my book to your friends and family. I'd love it if you'd review the book for me on Amazon or Goodreads. Reviews are the best way to help others find my book. My author site on Amazon is: http://amzn.to/1h80f92

If you want to learn more about me, my books or my business, find me at:
http://www.denisekalm.com
http://www.dpkcoaching.com
http://www.kalmkreative.com

As a special offer, if you are struggling to get a bigger LinkedIn network, contact me and I can link you in with my sizable network. This will help you get going more quickly. For those who would like more personal career guidance, contact me and we can set up some coaching.

Again, thank you. You're the reason I do this writing, and you give meaning to my work.

Denise P. Kalm